Strictly Kiwi

Graham Hutchins

Hodder Moa

National Library of New Zealand Cataloguing-in-Publication Data
Hutchins, Graham.
Strictly Kiwi / Graham Hutchins.
ISBN 978-1-86971-142-9
1. Popular culture-New Zealand. 2. New Zealand-Social life
and customs. I. Title.
306.0993-dc 22

A Hodder Moa Book

Published in 2010 by Hachette New Zealand Ltd
4 Whetu Place, Mairangi Bay
Auckland, New Zealand

Text © Graham Hutchins 2010
The moral rights of the author have been asserted.
Design and format © Hachette New Zealand Ltd 2010

All rights reserved. No part of this publication may be reproduced or transmitted in any form or
by any means, electronic or mechanical, including photocopying, recording, or any information
storage and retrieval system, without permission in writing from the publisher.

Designed and produced by Hachette New Zealand Ltd
Printed by in China by Toppan Leefung Printing Ltd

The author wishes to acknowledge the assistance of Project Kiwiana, Otorohanga
(www.kiwianatown.co.nz).

FSC
Mixed Sources
Product group from well-managed
forests and other controlled sources
Cert no. SGS-COC-004105
www.fsc.org
© 1996 Forest Stewardship Council

Contents

Photographic Credits

Alexander Turnbull Library, National Library of New Zealand: Pages 13 & 23 (F-2461-1/4-MNZ, Weekly News Collection),
17 (F-1434-35mm-12A, Evening Post Collection), 19 (F-1117-1/4, John Pascoe Collection), 27 (19130-1/1), 31 (F-1485-1/4-MNZ, Making New Zealand Collection), 43 (F-52226-1/2, Petersen Collection), 44 (Eph-C-Alcohol-Hours-1948-3), 45 (PADL-000185, Evening Post Collection), 46 (Eph-C-Cabot-Music-1963-01), 48 (PAColl-8163-67, New Zealand Free Lance Collection), 50 (Eph-A-Show-Auckland-1880-01), 53 (114/275/20, Evening Post Collection), 55 (MNZ-1048-1/4-F), 56 (PADL-000329, Damer Farrell Collection), 60 (Eph-A-phono-1930-01-5), 61 (Eph-A-Maori-Concert-1930s-01), 63 (G-5870-1/1, James McAllister Collection), 104 (GG-12-1029, Gladys M Goodall Collection), 106 (PA12-5644-22, Paul Thompson Collection), 110 (), 111 (Eph-E-Rail-1940s-01), 113 (Eph-A-Aviation-Teal-1940-01), 118 (C-23125-1/2, New Zealand Free Lance Collection), 134 (Eph-C-Retail-Farmers-1956-01)

Fairfax: Page 122

Farmers Trading Company: Page 132

Goodman Fielder Ltd: Page 26

Heinz Wattie's: Page 33

Iain Leitch: Page 51 and 52

Lion Rock Licensing Ltd: Pages 14 and 15

Masport: Pages 70 and 71

Max Cryer: Page 59

Murray Ball: Pages 128 and 129

Museum of New Zealand Te Papa Tongarewa: Pages 20 (GH004972), 21 (GH004849), 30 (GH010066), 54 (Brian Brake), 62 (B.022502), 85 (GH004742), 115 (O.006623/06), 117 (CG001384)

My Chilly Bin/Belinda Osgood: Page 109

My Chilly Bin/Cherie Palmer: 123

My Chilly Bin/Dave Addison: Page 67

My Chilly Bin/Linda Herraman: Page73

My Chilly Bin/Michi Krauss: Pages 64 and 119

My Chilly Bin/Natalia Tellechea: Page 127

My Chilly Bin/Pippa de Court: Pages 108 and 124

My Chilly Bin/Rob Tucker: Pages 83, 87, 98

My Chilly Bin/Thysje Arthur: Page 65

My Chilly Bin/William Connell: Page 125

New Zealand Herald: Pages 139 and 141

Peter Bush: Page 120

Peter Janssen: Page 40

PhotoSport: Page 57

Rob Suisted/Naturespic: Page 8

Ron Palenski: Page 25

Sue Campbell: Page 16

Ted Bryant: Page 140

Yates: Page 81

Introduction

What is Kiwiana?

Strictly Kiwi presents some of what has made New Zealand unique: the people, pursuits, pastimes, places, products and possessions that Kiwis love to call their own — even if we borrowed them. This includes items related to home and garden, sport, music, rest and relaxation, food and drink, travel and holidays, shopping and industry, all persons, objects and activities that have been enjoyed, admired and loved, and so have been elevated in status in the national consciousness.

These things fall under the umbrella term of 'Kiwiana', and such items have been described as 'microcosms of New Zealand cultural history'. They are indeed signposts of a unique and evolving society long cast adrift from Mother England and Europe, yet separate from the objects and customs of Maori culture, which has had the advantage of a 600-year head start.

From around the 1980s Pakeha New Zealanders began to feel the need to identify and celebrate traditions and objects that were neither British nor Maori (although often borrowing from both) and which were associated strongly with New Zealand. If that meant claiming a dessert dish conjured up out of egg whites and named after a Russian ballerina, then so be it.

The word Kiwiana began to be heard around the mid-1950s and was even going to be registered as a trademark in 1980. Typically, given New Zealanders' historical reticence, 'cultural cringe' and abhorrence of 'tall poppies' in an egalitarian land, the Kiwiana registration was not completed, leaving the word open for general use. That in itself was an indictment (or celebration) of our 'she'll be right', relaxed attitude and sheep-like behaviour. Indeed sheep have been legitimised as a Kiwiana item too.

Kiwiana is a funny bird. Deciding what it encompasses is not an exact science .While some purists may argue that local origin is paramount,

KIWIANA AHEAD

a widening view now accepts that common usage is equally important. Some may feel a little cheated to learn that bungy jumping was not invented out the back of the central North Island hill country, as gumbooted sheep farmers dived from great heights off limestone bluffs. But we adapted bungy jumping (from the custom of the Pentecost Islanders of Vanuatu) and took it to the world, before setting up operations Down Under that make the practice, after little more than 20 years, seem as Kiwi as corrugated iron, the bloke's shed, jandals, *Footrot Flats*, the Buzzy Bee — and our national bird, the kiwi.

The word Kiwiana was derived originally from the kiwi, of course, a creature unique to New Zealand, which, with its rather bizarre habits and physical characteristics, has been described as 'a bird designed by a committee'. The committee approach, with its egalitarian, consultative manner, is, appropriately, typical of the 'Kiwi' or New Zealand way of life too.

The kiwi is flightless, nocturnal, largely sightless, has plumage that is more hair-like than feather-like and features nostrils at the end of a long bill. As such it is regarded, along with items like the silver fern, as pure Kiwiana, in a purist definition that regards Kiwiana as icons of popular culture that originated in this country. Yet Kiwiana includes many things that fall beyond such strictures.

Rugby, racing and beer, for example, the popular 'trifecta' of post-World War II New Zealand, is made up of a game invented in England, a four-legged sideshow from all corners of the globe, and a hop-flavoured brew favoured by Europeans and Britons. Yet Kiwis played rugby so well that foreigners still believe the game originated here, and between the 1930s and 1960s we were the third highest beer imbibers on earth. Such has been our affinity with beer that it is reasonable to suppose that it was discovered in an Otago bush encampment full of thirsty tree-fellers.

So what qualified as Kiwiana took on varying dimensions over the years. From pop culture items such as toys, clothing and branded foods, Kiwiana soon embraced New Zealand icons, including people, places and events.

In recent years several celebratory books on Kiwiana have been produced. Many museums now boast Kiwiana sections and displays. Otorohanga, a small King Country town where, fittingly, New Zealand's first Kiwi House was created, has recently become doubly noteworthy as the Kiwiana capital of New Zealand.

Kiwiana is not yet a university subject, but such is the burgeoning popularity of the phenomenon that a Bachelor of Kiwiana (BK) may become a standard undergraduate degree. And that degree itself, further along the Kiwiana evolutionary chain, could join Marlborough sauvignon blanc, white water rafting and boy racers as legitimate mid-21st century entries on the list of Kiwiana.

I hope *Strictly Kiwi* stirs some warm memories and whimsical ponderings — and let's you fluff up your Kiwi feathers.

Our Symbols

The Kiwi

Flightless and shy but at least it's ours

The kiwi has been taken to the collective heart of New Zealanders, so much so that local inhabitants — Maori, Pakeha and any other group that feels sufficiently assimilated to call New Zealand home — are now referred to as Kiwis.

Because of New Zealand's extended prehistoric physical isolation from the rest of the world, a distinctive fauna developed. There were few predatory mammals and, as a result, a bird like the kiwi was able to evolve as a flightless, ground-dwelling species. Evidence of wings can be found on the kiwi but there was no evolutionary compulsion for them to develop. A long bill with nostrils at the tip, a unique feature, developed though, to facilitate the kiwi's search for food in the soil and leaf litter. Kiwis are also nocturnal and have poor sight. They rely on other features, particularly their strategically placed nostrils and acute sense of hearing. Their plumage is more like hair than feathers and, when compared with other birds, they are regarded as slightly odd. The fact that the kiwi lays large eggs (its eggs are bigger in relation to body size than any other known species) is another example of the kiwi's distinctiveness.

Kiwis flourished in New Zealand for 30 million years, generally fossicking around the forest floor at night, in an unencumbered state, until

humans arrived. The latter brought rats, cats, dogs, stoats and possums — predators that found the kiwi easy game — and with extensive land clearing the kiwi's natural environment was further compromised. By the 1990s the kiwi was in trouble. Numbers in the North, South and Stewart Islands had dwindled to the extent that conservation programmes became critical to the birds' survival.

In earlier times, New Zealanders were known as En Zedders, Maorilanders and Fernlanders, but these days they are proud to call themselves Kiwis.

World War I is cited as the pivotal event that saw New Zealand troops become known as Kiwis, the nickname generated by the soldiers' generous use of Kiwi Boot Polish — ironically an Australian product, introduced in 1906 by William Ramsay, and named 'Kiwi' to honour his wife's country of origin.

Kiwis — New Zealanders — delighted in championing the underdog, certainly in earlier decades, and probably because of our position as occupants of a small country at the end of the world, we often saw ourselves as underdogs too — just like the kiwi which was uniquely ours, and which, once the predators arrived, was up against it.

This attitude and national characteristic was transferred to the sporting field, notably in the case of the All Blacks rugby team who became famous for fighting rearguard actions and winning many games narrowly after coming from behind.

The kiwi, though, was losing its battle and in safeguarding its survival developed traits that saw it develop ostrich-like tactics. It was now 'head in the sand' time and these tendencies, too, were identified, perhaps unkindly, as behaviours that could be assigned to New Zealanders. We were described as 'passionless' and 'ostrich-like' for a time, particularly during the 'she'll be right' years when we were living high on the sheep's back.

Since those heady days of the 1950s and 1960s, New Zealanders have had to develop a certain passion and fight rearguard actions which, if nothing else, made our nickname, Kiwis, appropriate again.

The small King Country town of Otorohanga has become something of a Mecca for Kiwis for here the kiwi can be viewed throughout the day in a faithfully created 'natural' environment, in the country's first Kiwi House. Many overseas tourists visit the 'shrine' to the kiwi too, in a town that prides itself, with every justification, on being the 'Kiwiana' town of New Zealand.

Silver Fern

Symbolism in silver

The Silver Fern used to be the name of a steel-framed railcar that trundled between Auckland and Wellington on the North Island Main Trunk. These days the national netball team are called the Silver Ferns.

Obviously the silver fern has come to be regarded as a national symbol, often as well known as the kiwi. It has been our sporting emblem since the days of the 1888 New Zealand Natives rugby team when the fern leaf appeared on players' jerseys during the course of their 100-plus game itinerary. In fact, from that time, the silver fern has emerged as a more generalised emblem, featuring on our dairy exports, and in 1956, being included in a revised national Coat of Arms.

In the very early days of European settlement New Zealand was covered in bush, and ferns were a common component of the vegetation-clad landscape. The attractive silver fern, with dark green upper surface and a striking silver underside to its fronds, caught the eye of early settlers, and it was little surprise when it

was adopted as emblems on early newspaper front pages, military and sporting badges and more utilitarian objects like tobacco tins.

The silver fern is the official plant of New Zealand. Its botanical name, *Cyathea dealbata*, is typically less well known. In Maori it is ponga, and from this New Zealanders have come to call all tree ferns 'pungas'. Maori used the fronds to mark trails, as moonlight reflected off the upturned silver side.

In the twenty-first century the silver fern has taken on quasi-religious significance because of its appearance on All Blacks jerseys. Other sub-cultures like the art world have also recognised the icon. Frederick Hundertwasser's proposal for a new national flag which would be dominated by an impressionistic green coil or koru based on the burgeoning fern frond, set against a silver background, honours the symbolic importance of the silver fern.

The silver fern has graced the All Blacks jersey for over 100 years.

Growing Up

Buzzy Bee

From New Lynn to New York

The Buzzy Bee is regarded as one of the most readily recognised pieces of Kiwiana, yet its origins are somewhat clouded. In 1931 at the New York City Toy Fair, newly founded toy company Fisher-Price produced a range of new toys including Bark Puppy, Drummer-Bear and Dizzy Rino. In 1950 they produced a toy similar to the Buzzy Bee. So some Kiwiana pundits have suggested that the Buzzy Bee owes its origins to the USA and Fisher-Price.

Be that as it may, the Buzzy Bee and its origins, are popularly credited to the efforts of Hec and John Ramsey, Auckland brothers who began producing the clacking marvel on a string in the mid-1940s. The Ramseys started out modestly enough, manufacturing wooden cores for toilet roll holders, before turning their hands to more creative wooden pursuits. Hec Ramsey produced the popular Mary Lou doll in 1941, before coming up with Oscar Ostrich, Richard Rabbit and Dorable Duck.

After World War II, John Ramsey designed the Buzzy Bee and with New Zealand's strict post-war import licences limiting incoming toys, the Buzzy Bee sold in the thousands. Later

14

additions to the wooden toy stable included Kris Cricket, Peter Pup and Playful Puss.

Buzzy Bee remained the favourite though. With its distinctive clack-clack sound as it was pulled or pushed and its bold colours, it was difficult not to notice the iconic wooden toy in thousands of Kiwi homes and backyards — unless you were the father of the house and had just arrived home from the six o'clock swill, unsteady of gait and blurred of vision. In such situations undignified tumbles, sparked by Buzzy Bees 'left lying around', led to admonishments. Some Buzzy Bees suffered a cruel fate if they had been left outside in the long lawn grass as the light faded. Six o'clock

swillers, in an attempt at atonement, sometimes took to the lawns after a re-heated dinner, only to snag on the kids' favourite toy.

Following its heyday, the Buzzy Bee operation passed through several manufacturers' hands and now rests with Lion Rock Ventures. In a concession to increasing global influences the Buzzy Bee, once confined to the Kiwi market, is now made in China and has been released on the international market.

The Buzzy Bee was never meant to fly, but it did — in the cargo holds of jet aircraft. It is a far cry from its humble, flightless beginnings in a New Lynn factory.

The Buzzy Bee range from the 1950s: Buzzy Bee (far left) and from left below Elle-gator, Driver Don, Dorable Duck and her Ducklings.

Plunket

Cornerstone of the welfare state

TO HELP THE MOTHERS — AND SAVE THE BABIES

The Plunket Society, or the New Zealand Society for the Health of Women and Children, was founded in 1907 at a time when the country's reputation for quality infant care was low. The name Plunket derived from the wife of the Governor-General Lord Plunket, an influential supporter of the ground-breaking society.

Prior to 1907 New Zealand society assumed that mothers knew instinctively how to nurture their offspring. Bottle feeding had replaced breastfeeding, despite the lack of knowledge of nourishing milk formulas. Sugary mixes or unadulterated cow's milk were fed to infants with subsequent digestive upsets and a worrying mortality rate. In the early 1900s close to 8 percent of New Zealand's annual newborns died before their first birthday.

Dr Frederic Truby King, a Dunedin medical superintendent, was the pioneer who first recognised the need for better infant care. He concocted a milk preparation that duplicated the nutritional value of mothers' milk.

Branches of the Plunket Society sprang up throughout the

country and for many years the name Plunket, and Karitane nurses, became synonymous with a caring society that supported mothers and infants and advocated not only a healthy diet but plenty of exercise, fresh air and sunshine.

By the early 1940s, New Zealand had become the Welfare State, the 'social laboratory' of the world in terms of how to look after those least able to look after themselves. Infants and children were included in this group and free milk in schools and state funded dental and medical programmes were instituted as New Zealand's 'cradle to grave' welfare state mantra resonated.

The Plunket Book, first introduced in the 1920s, became a Kiwi icon in its own right. It charted weight gains, developmental milestones and care requirements (including pivotal bowel training regimes), for newborn New Zealanders.

The Plunket Society was responsible for reducing the country's infant death rate to the lowest in the world, at a time when it could be postulated that New Zealand was 'the best place in the world to raise children'.

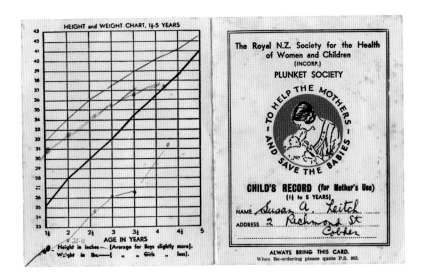

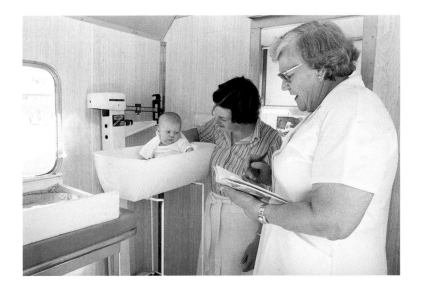

Right: A 'mobile Plunket nurse' weighs a baby.

Dental Nurses

Murder house of horrors

At a time when the state took a more active role in the health and general well-being of children, the emergence of dental nurses was much-heralded.

The introduction of the School Dental Service in 1921 came about as a result of the deplorable state of New Zealanders' teeth at the beginning of the twentieth century. The service was singularly successful in improving the oral health of children, although most kids were prepared to contemplate having tooth decay if it meant avoiding the often painful drilling of teeth to accommodate fillings. Treadle drills were much feared, for their impetus relied on the leg-power and co-ordination of the dental nurse.

Woe betide any kid who had to endure the treadle machine wielded by an inexperienced dental nurse grad.

By the 1960s electric drills had improved the efficiency of tooth drilling, but the little white dental clinic was still known to most kids as the 'murder house'.

For many years New Zealand adults expected to have all or most of their teeth extracted as they matured. Poor teeth were considered almost like male pattern baldness in men who were unlucky enough to inherit the baldness gene. Matters like poor diet, important trace elements missing from water supplies, and shoddy dental hygiene — not the inevitability of growing older — had left many New Zealanders with some of the worst teeth in the world. Dentures or the toothless, gummy look were de rigueur before government authorities stepped in.

The setting up of dental care for New Zealand troops during World War I proved that the notion of a state-run dental service could be translated to peacetime at home. The success of Plunket nurses proved that women could be deployed by government agencies and sent out to provide assistance in the field for newborns and mothers. While there was resistance from the dental establishment, made up of professional men (who feared the incursion of hastily trained dental quacks), there was no reason the Plunket model wouldn't work.

When Colonel Thomas Hunter, former director of military dental services, was appointed Chief Dental Officer in the Department of Health in 1920, changes were set in place. A team of dental nurses specialising in the care of first teeth were trained for two years before being dispatched far and wide to the nation's primary schools.

There was no comparable system anywhere else in the world and Colonel Hunter's scheme was controversial, but its eventual success was unequivocal. By 1927 nearly 20,000 primary school children were treated at dental clinics by over 40 trained nurses. By 1978 the figures were over 600,000 primary and pre-school children, and 1255 nurses.

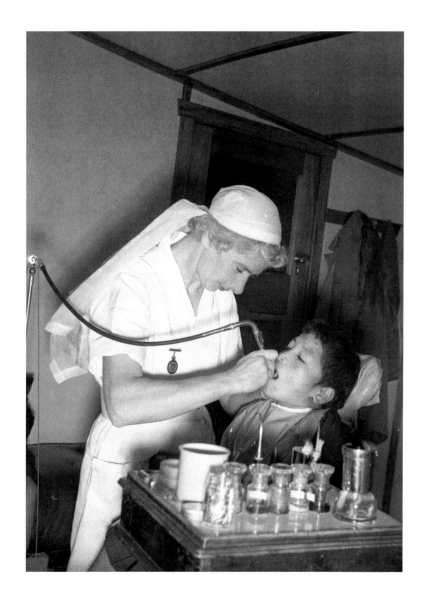

A school dental nurse treats a pupil of Te Kaha School, 1944.

Fun Ho! Toys

For toy boys and girls

A Wellingtonian named Jack Underwood began producing moulded lead toys in his basement in the 1930s. With Fun Ho! as his brand name Underwood eventually turned his hand to full-time toy making and after branching out and establishing a non-ferrous foundry providing metal componentry for the World War II effort, he continued to dabble in toy manufacture.

By now Underwood was making cast-aluminium toys based on British and American cast iron novelties. With wartime restrictions and later import limitations, Fun Ho! toys ruled the New Zealand roost. The company, seeking more space, moved to New Plymouth, then down the road to Inglewood, where the company soon became well-known as 'Underwood of Inglewood'. In the 1960s the company introduced zinc-cast toys called Fun Ho! midgets.

Models of fire-trucks, tractors, racing cars and other wheeled objects beloved of small boys (and girls) in sand-pits became icons of the 'golden weather' years. Fun Ho! toys fitted Kiwi kids' landscape and needs — and that of their parents. They were rugged, long-lasting survivors of the decades following World War II when the wartime manufacturing ethos led to products built to last or withstand a shell blast.

Although the company expanded into furniture, tricycles, bicycles and pedal cars, the 1970s witnessed the lifting of import restrictions and soon cheap, plastic toys rendered Fun Ho! toys less attractive. By 1982 toy production stopped and in 1987 the factory ceased operations altogether.

Today surviving Fun Ho! toys are well regarded as collectors' items by lovers of Kiwiana and collectibles. The Fun Ho! name also lives on in the Fun Ho! National Toy Museum located appropriately at Inglewood. A range of 100 toys, at any one time, is still made today at the museum foundry using the original Fun Ho! moulding plates.

A Fun Ho! toy road grader (opposite) and van, both from the 1940s.

School Milk

Ten o'clock closing

At 10 am daily, on the dot, half-pint milk bottles in wire crates were presented to New Zealand school kids for drinking. The practice was a distinctly Kiwi phenomenon and continued for 30 years, from its inception in 1937. Free school milk was the brainchild of Peter Fraser, the Labour Government's Minister of Health.

Supplying milk to schools, in respect of its benefits, was sometimes controversial, but after the Health Department in 1920 had isolated health deficiencies in school kids, including a generally scrawny demeanour, the idea carried considerable merit.

George Bernard Shaw, the Irish playwright, visited New Zealand in 1934 at a time when the country was becoming a 'social laboratory', free of class constraints. Shaw advocated egalitarian options like free school milk as part of a fair welfare state in which our ready supply of milk could be put to good advantage.

Through the 1940s and 1950s and into the 1960s, school kids continued drinking their half-pint of school milk although, in truth, it was often warm; semi-curdled even. But the earlier health ravages of the 1918 flu epidemic, the polio scare and poor dietary outcomes from even poorer households during the Depression years had led to impoverishment and malnutriton.

It was never truly established that the daily slug of milk covered all nourishment bases, but it was a start. As the country climbed beyond the privations of earlier decades and the health of school kids improved, New Zealand's reputation as 'the best place in the world to raise kids' — a land of milk and honey, no less — carried increased credibility.

By 1967 New Zealand's prosperous, healthy society rendered the need for school milk redundant. The ten o'clock supply of bottles was canned. It had done its job. The health of school kids had blossomed. Ironically, in the same year — 1967 — ten o'clock closing for grown-ups at the pub was also introduced. That didn't mean that fathers no longer had to glug back a half-pint of milk too, but simply that hotels could now close their doors at 10 pm, rather than the six o'clock closing of the notorious six o'clock swill era.

Auckland school children drinking their free daily milk, 1939.

'Blue Smoke'
A haunting melody and smoky vocals

'Blue Smoke' was written by Ruru Karaitiana, an easy-going Maori bloke from Dannevirke, on the troop ship *Aquitania*, which was carrying him to the Middle East during World War II. Before the war, Karaitiana had learned to play guitar, ukulele, piano and trombone by ear, and because of such innate musicality, 'Blue Smoke', inspired by the funnel smoke of the troop ship, came to him naturally.

The song was performed at troop concerts, but despite its obvious merit and charm, London publishers were not interested. After the war, Karaitiana was able to interest Tanza Records who released the song on 78 rpm, a record claimed to be the first produced in its entirety in New Zealand. With suitable smoky vocals from Pixie Williams the record went on to sell 50,000 copies. It appealed to post-war New Zealand because of its relaxed, atmospheric mood and, despite its Hawaiian ambience created largely by the use of steel guitar in the instrumental accompaniment, it had a decidedly Kiwi twang and tang.

The wartime lyrics spoke of nostalgia for home and now that the war was over the sentiment was all the more meaningful for a New Zealand society licking its emotional wounds.

The Radio Corporation of New Zealand had had a lot to do with the final release of

'Blue Smoke' to the general populace. They set up New Zealand's first local record company, Tanza (To Assist New Zealand Artists), at a time when His Master's Voice (HMV), the leading phonograph company, showed scant interest in recording home-grown talent.

'Blue Smoke' was such a haunting melody that soon international artists like Al Morgan, Dean Martin, Teddy Phillips and Leslie Howard recorded versions on major labels. Anne Zeigler and Webster Booth even recorded a duet of the song. In 1951, the song was among the best-selling music in the US. Dean Martin contacted Karaitiana, seeking a follow-up.

In the New Zealand scheme of things, Karaitiana had soon had his fifteen minutes of fame and he eventually went back to working seasons in the Dannevirke and Dunedin freezing works, although he still performed at dance halls playing in a five-piece band. 'Blue Smoke' had definitely drifted by.

The sheet music for Ruru Karaitiana's classic song was published in 1947.

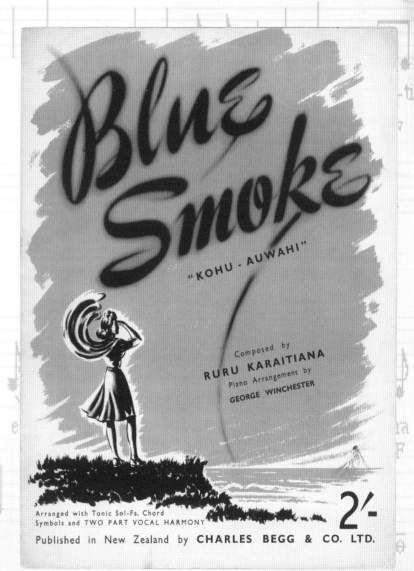

Food & Drink

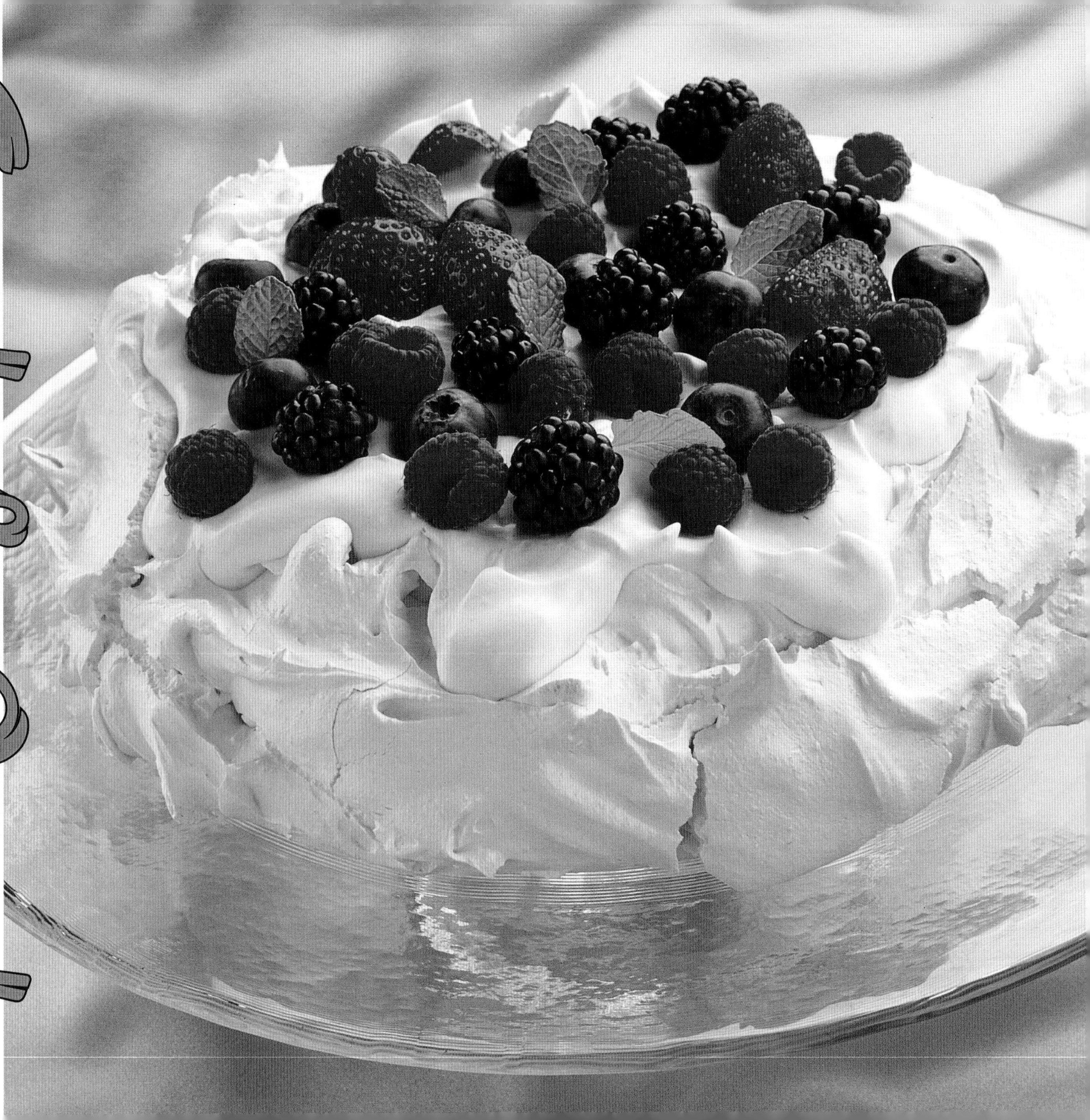

Pavlova

Making the 'perfect pav'

Out in the Kiwi hinterland the making of the perfect pavlova has, over the years, been attended with much ceremony. Indeed the making and baking of any sort of pavlova has, for many New Zealand women, created insecurity.

So what is this dessert dish that has presented such tension? The pavlova is essentially a meringue-based sweet concoction made up of egg whites, vinegar, vanilla essence, caster sugar and cornflour. The traditional New Zealand pavlova features slices of kiwifruit adorning the generous covering of whipped cream that completes the dessert, although strawberries and other fruit items can be used.

The dish was inspired by Russian ballerina Anna Pavlova, who toured New Zealand in 1925–26. She also toured Australia which led to further anxiety. The Australians claimed the pavlova as their own, despite New Zealanders nominating it as their national dessert. Various Australian

Anna Pavlova dancing in Wellington.

sources make the claim that a Perth chef was the first person to make a pavlova, although Anna Pavlova's biographer, among others, cited a Wellington hotel chef as the first cook to come up with the somewhat controversial dish.

The Wellington chef had seen Pavlova dressed in a tutu covered in cabbage roses constructed from green silk, and, true to his calling, was inspired to concoct a dish that best reflected Pavlova's exotic outfit. In the chef's eye, the meringue shell represented the tutu and the whipped cream the tutu's net. The roses were depicted by slices of kiwifruit (known as Chinese gooseberries back then).

The country-wide infatuation with Anna Pavlova may have led to the often solemn business of making the 'perfect pav' in New Zealand. Some women deigned to attempt its concoction, although the drifts of whipped cream were often used to cover design and construction flaws — like the cracking of the outer shell.

The presence of the 'perfect pav', gracing down-country spreads and suppers, is a distinctively Kiwi phenomenon.

Pavlova Recipe

4 egg whites
375 g (13 oz) sugar
1 teaspoon vanilla essence
1 teaspoon vinegar
1 tablespoon cornflour

Turn the oven on to 180°C (350°F). Beat the egg whites and sugar until very thick and glossy. Add the vanilla essence, vinegar and cornflour and beat again. Cover an oven tray with baking paper and place the pavlova mixture in the centre. Spread or shape into a 20-cm circle. Place in the oven and turn the temperature down to 100°C (210°F). Bake for 1 hour, then turn the oven off and open the door slightly. Leave the pavlova in the oven until it is cold, then remove and decorate with whipped cream and fruit.

Chesdale Cheese

Triangular cheddar

At a time when refrigeration had yet to become commonplace, the emergence of Chesdale cheese was eminently pragmatic. The triangular cheese segments kept well, had a smooth, smoky flavour, and a certain novelty value, particularly for children, who often found the triangular, individually wrapped portions in their lunch boxes. The processed cheese would keep for long periods of time in the cupboard whereas standard cheese had a habit of turning into a monster once it had been cut into — it developed mould, took on a strong odour, and cracked and sweated before drying out.

Chesdale first hit the market in block form. Because it was rindless, proponents could legitimately make the claim that there was no waste. Later the distinctive small foil-wrapped triangular portions evolved. There was no logical reason — to laymen and women at least — why cheese now came in triangular form, but there is no doubting its popularity with kids, many of whom had eschewed cheese in general.

A catchy advertising campaign that starred two down-country farm characters called Ches and Dale, singing a promotional song about being the 'boys from down on the farm', became a Kiwi standard. Ches and Dale first appeared in the 1960s, dressed in rural garb including gumboots and black singlets. The invention of graphic artists Dick Frizzell and Sam Harvey, they first appeared on TV in 1965.

New Zealand Butter

'Better Butter'

Large-scale dairy farming and butter production were twentieth century developments. Earlier a certain amount of butter had been made available to the shipping trade and some was exported to Australia. Usually, though, New Zealand butter was absorbed by the local market and it was not regarded as being significant to the national economy.

Refrigeration helped change the face of butter production and increased export quantities. Further developments like the cream separator, milking machines and quality control practices like herd testing and pasteurisation put dairying on the front foot.

As New Zealand developed into an agricultural stronghold, dairy farming emerged as a vital component. Soon farmers were making their own butter and eventually butter factories began sprouting on the dairying lowlands. Such was the butter bounty that a lucrative export market developed.

Inevitably, given New Zealand's pre-eminent export dairying industry, New Zealand butter developed an international reputation. The brand name 'Anchor' has long been associated with butter from New Zealand, a product known for its richness and consistency. Despite postulations that the name 'Anchor' derived from the export ships' anchors, this is not so. A Waikato farmer known as Henry Reynolds had a worker who sported a tattoo of an anchor and Reynolds decided to adopt 'Anchor' as the name for his butter. The New Zealand Dairy Association later bought Reynolds' creamery and the 'Anchor' brand and in 1919 the National Co-Operative Dairy Company acquired it.

Despite the hit butter took in the 1960s and 1970s when its high cholesterol content led to the development of margarine as a reputedly safer, more artery-friendly alternative, the creamier taste of butter has brought resurgence in use in recent years.

New Zealand is the largest exporter of dairy products. Foreigners equate this country with icons such as the All Blacks, mutton, All Blacks, bungy jumping, Vegemite, All Blacks and butter.

The traditional block of butter survives (albeit in metric measurement), although dramatic rises in the price of butter on the local market in recent years have made it virtually a luxury item.

In earlier times the mind-numbing routine of hand-milking cows twice a day made dairying a less than attractive proposition. However, by 1919 half of New Zealand's herds were milked by machine and by the early 1950s very few weren't.

Opposite: A butter box made from kahikatea.
Above: Grading butter at an Auckland factory, 1930s.

Wattie's

Waste not

In the early 1930s James Wattie became aware that a lot of the fruit and vegetable bounty produced on the fertile sunny Heretaunga Plains in Hawke's Bay was going to waste. He conceived the idea of a cannery to take advantage. Thousands of jobs were created when J Wattie Canneries began business in Hastings, not only in the cannery process but also in growing and merchandising at either end of the operation.

Soon new crops were being grown in Hawke's Bay, which became known as the 'fruit bowl of New Zealand', specifically for canning at the new cannery. Green peas were one of the early favourites, but eventually Wattie's also became synonymous in New Zealand with canned fruit salad, soup, asparagus, peaches and two perennials, perhaps New Zealand's best-known instant meals — baked beans and spaghetti. Wattie's tomato sauce was another product that developed iconic status.

In the early 1930s, 80 percent of New Zealand's canned food was imported. By the time James Wattie retired in 1972, New Zealand was self-sufficient in fruit and vegetables and had, moreover, become a significant exporter of such goods.

Wattie's was an innovator. It was the first to produce quick frozen foods in New Zealand and their pioneering pet food operation emerged from a desire to utilise the fish waste from fish processing for humans. Felix for cats and Fido for dogs were pioneering outcomes. It has been reported that such was the newness of the pet food notion, and such was its flavour, that a few Kiwis who had come through the standard 'two wars and a depression' tucked in, much to the horror of pet cats and dogs. And in keeping with historical folklore regarding such things it was pointed out that James Wattie was of Scottish extraction. Nothing would go to waste — just as it had been the sight of rotting produce in Hawke's Bay in summer (the locals couldn't keep up) that inspired his cannery empire in the first place.

The line from an old advertising jingle 'It must be Wattie's', resonated through New Zealand in the 1950s and 1960s. These days Wattie's is part of the global HJ Heinz group. but still based in Hastings, and now with around 1200 product lines.

Right: The Wattie's product range in the mid 1950s.

Tip Top Ice Cream

Do the hokey pokey

In a land that was inundated with cream and dairy products it was no surprise that ice-cream became a Kiwi favourite. New Zealand ranks third in the world for ice-cream consumption and the Tip Top label has become the standard bearer.

New Zealand's first ice-cream was made by hand and sold, appropriately, from portable hand carts. In 1935 two Dunedin vendors moved to Wellington to set up the country's first milkbar which sold ice-cream and milkshakes and nothing else. Len Malaghan and Bert Hayman, on the look-out for a name for their new venture, overheard a conversation in a restaurant that included the vernacular compliment 'tip top' in describing an excellent meal. 'Tip Top' it was, and by the end of the decade Tip Top milkbars had extended to the south of the North Island and the north of the South Island.

By the 1950s the ice-cream industry had grown to such an extent that New Zealand had over 100 ice-cream companies. Many of the names reflected the iced, snowing aspect of the new product that had swept the country: Westland Snowflake, Everest, Arctic, Glacier and Alpine. Even small towns like Waipukurau, Taumarunui and Huntly had their own ice-cream factories.

In 1939 Tip Top arrived in Auckland, and by 1951 their factories in Auckland and Wellington were producing the equivalent of no less than 55 million ice-creams annually. General Foods took over Tip Top and when, in 1960, the two independently operated factories in Auckland and Wellington were combined, Tip Top accounted for 55 percent of New Zealand's ice cream production. By 1988 Tip Top controlled 60 percent of the market.

Along the way Tip Top produced such iced and ice-creamy novelties as the TT2, Tip Toppa, Choc Bar, Fru Ju, Moggy Man, Toppa, Topsy and Trumpet, as well as a wide range of flavours for their cone-based wares. Included in the latter was something called 'Hokey Pokey'. It is generally accepted that New Zealand gave the world hokey pokey ice-cream. The Meadowgold Ice Cream Company of Papatoetoe, Auckland, first sold the ground-breaking concoction (basic vanilla ice-cream containing chunks of toffee) in the 1940s before Tip Top made the flavour famous in the 1950s.

The practice of adding toffee to ice-cream wasn't new, but the distinctive taste of hokey pokey chunks, made for a taste and texture explosion that, cashing in on its unique sugar, golden syrup and bicarbonate of soda recipe, helped fill the Tip Top coffers.

Today TipTop is still in tip-top shape owned by New Zealand dairy giant Fonterra.

Enough for everyone in the new Tip Top half gallon pack

Tip Top's new half gallon packs are made especially for expected appetites or unexpected guests. Each pack is packed with creamy smooth Vanilla, Hokey Pokey, Strawberry or Rainbow ice cream. With recipes printed on the pack, every half gallon you buy is full of dessert ideas too.

Vegemite/Marmite

'Too much spoils the flavour'

For many years New Zealanders often thought that Marmite contained meat, and vegemite didn't. Ironically the New Zealand manufacturers of Marmite, Sanitarium, are Seventh Day Adventists and, as such, vegetarian. In this country, Marmite has always been advertised as a vegetable or yeast extract, but still the confusion remained.

Some of the confusion may have originated when British meat extracts like OXO were introduced to the world, virtually at the same time that Marmite was first exported to New Zealand from England. In the 1920s, despite an abundance of real meat, local firms had churned out their own meat extracts too. BOVO from Hellaby's of Auckland, Bovine from a Dunedin company and Carnox beef essence from P.O. Manufacturing Co, Wellington, were particularly popular. In the 1940s New Zealand began producing its own Marmite.

Partly because of these factors the Marmite as meat myth gained ground. After all, Marmite did taste a bit like meat extract.

Vegemite, based on Marmite, was, as imputed by name, decidedly meat-less. It was first made in New Zealand in 1958 out of yeast and vegetable matter like celery and onion extract. Despite the fact it was invented in Australia, Kiwis took to it in spade-fills and it remains more popular here than there. New Zealanders account for over two million jars a year.

Be it Marmite or Vegemite, the concentrated extracts have been regarded as acquired tastes. In earlier times, users were advised to spread the stuff sparingly for 'too much spoils the flavour'. The extracts did not enjoy much success in the USA where consumers were in the habit of smearing their spreads too generously, but in New Zealand, with more conservative applications, Marmite and Vegemite sandwiches have become Kiwi staples.

Opposite: The modern Vegemite jar.
Right: The lid of a 1940s New Zealand Marmite jar and a Marmite advertisment from the late 1960s.

Tea

The last cuppa

In New Zealand tea was as English as a 'good cuppa'. Wherever English colonists went they took tea with them. New Zealand, with its often quoted 'more English than the English' persona, was destined to take tea to its heart and parts further south.

Tea was regarded as both a panacea and a pick-me-up. It could calm the nerves and, in virtually the same cupful, invigorate. At times of national crisis Mum put the kettle on. When it was time to mark joyous occasions — like the All Blacks beating the Springboks in 1956 — Mum put the same kettle on. In between times when there was a lull and a certain colonial dullness descended, a good cup of tea was again called for.

In times of local calamity, like the day the postman fell off his bike and left his front teeth embedded in the asphalt, the first person on the scene was not the St John's Ambulance driver or local doctor but the woman at number 36 with a brimming mug of Bell tea.

The popular tea brand names were simple enough, although back at the turn of the twentieth century, asking for Brown Barrett and Company's Colombo Garden Heliotrope variety was enough to render the buyer in need of a good cuppa.

In the early 1930s Kiwis were drinking an estimated 200 million cups of Bell tea on an annual basis and by the late 1980s the same easy-to-remember brand accounted for 30 percent of New Zealand tea sales. Close behind Bell tea was the Choysa brand introduced away back in the 1900s. Bushells was another high achiever and when it was endorsed by radio personality Aunt Daisy its stocks rose.

Advertising jingles and slogans became almost as popular and recognisable as the teas themselves. Roma tea claimed to be the 'dust-free' tea. The early 1950s' wits indulged in a certain word-play with the promotional mantra and came up with 'Roma — the tea-free dust', although Roma was as worthy as any brew.

After World War II tea lost some of its allure for younger generations who came to view tea-drinking as a fetish of the establishment. Besides, coffee was now making in-roads and in the following decades, coffee bars and the emergence of instant coffee consigned tea to the back-burner for many. However, during the youth revolution of the 1960s it was suggested that the tannin in tea was, if not mind-expanding, then mildly mood-elevating and/or tranquillising. As such, tea enjoyed a minor resurgence. Some young thrill-seekers even smoked it in an acrid attempt to 'get high'.

The Tea Council of New Zealand attempted to re-brand tea as the basis for 'tea-raves' for the Beatle generation. Iced tea became popular and the development of tea bags made tea-making more 'instant' in a speeded-up lifestyle. In this day and age, with the introduction of tea houses, attempts have been made to challenge coffee's dominance but the increasing pace of life seems better served by the caffeine rush of coffee than the contemplative tannin-fix of tea. Indeed for new generations the 'last cuppa' happened some time ago.

Older Kiwis still enjoy the ceremony of putting the kettle on and waiting for the brew to do its magic and settle in the tea pot. Some still swear by the need to rotate the tea pot four times before pouring, and other time-consuming rituals.

Lemon & Paeroa

Bubbling up from down under

No drink is more Kiwi-oriented than the combination of mineral water, from an archetypical small town on the edge of the Hauraki Plains, and lemon extract.

Lemon and Paeroa, or L&P, was originally based on spring water that bubbled to the surface in a Paeroa paddock in the 1880s. Eventually, the Paeroa Natural Mineral Water Company was formed to bottle the water, which had already been enjoyed by locals, who often inserted a wedge of lemon to augment what was regarded as more a tonic than a casual soft drink.

Tests had found significant amounts of magnesium carbonate, a medicinal trace element, in the water and in 1907 Menzies & Co. purchased Paeroa Natural Mineral Water Co. Soon lemon was added to the water. The new

Paeroa's big L&P bottle — world famous in New Zealand.

owners became Grey and Menzies as casks of water were transported to its Auckland factory. Such logistics were expensive and when the water was further analysed and its salts identified, it was discovered that such elements could be added to ordinary water anywhere. The Paeroa spring was no longer pivotal.

In 1963 Grey & Menzies merged with C.L. Innes Ltd. The outcome was Innes Tartan Ltd. In 1964 the latter was bought out by L.D. Nathan Ltd who built the imposing Oasis bottling facility at Mount Wellington, where L&P, Coca-Cola and Schweppes products were manufactured and bottled.

Coca-Cola remains the most popular soft drink in New Zealand, but Lemon and Paeroa still makes up a significant percentage of the market. And tourists can be excused for thinking that L&P still comes from Paeroa. At the intersection of State Highways 2 and 26 in the heart of the Thames Valley town, a 7-metre-high bottle of L&P celebrates New Zealand's most famous home-produced soft drink.

The old and the new: L&P bottles from the early sixties (note the 'Innes Tarten' label) and today.

Beer

When SOS stood for six o'clock swill

Beer. No beverage in New Zealand's history has created so much controversy, unless it was the hard liquor of the early pioneer days, or home-made high-proof hooch or flagrant abuse of cheap supermarket wine in the early twenty-first century.

Until countries like Germany sneaked ahead, no country drank more beer per head of population than Kiwis. Beer was as English as tea and for that reason was always destined to catch on in the colony, where hard manual labour aimed at breaking in the new country led to prodigious thirsts. The term 'manual labour' was significant for it was the men who gravitated to the after-work keg and quart bottles of earlier times. The women, often aghast at the drunken outcomes, stuck to tea.

Symbolically, Captain James Cook produced New Zealand's first brew, a challenging concoction of molasses and rimu leaves that purportedly limited the risk of scurvy. Some say it brought it on.

In 1835 New Zealand's first brewery was established by Joel Polack at Kororareka. Significantly, it was the first European industry set up in the new country. Breweries sprouted in the newly established towns and work camps and when New Zealand's gold rushes erupted the breweries cashed in. There was no one thirstier than a hard-working miner, either about to celebrate a rich alluvial return or drown sorrows and frustration. Thames, scene of gold rushes in the 1860s, boasted 80 hotels, and towns like Greymouth, Hokitika and Westport seemed to have more hotels than shops.

Breweries and pubs sprang up everywhere. Eventually, as the years passed and improved roading and transport increased, rationalisation produced fewer breweries. Earlier provincial breweries and their products became significant landmarks. Proof that Kiwis' dalliance with beer was not a passing fad — despite political agitation for prohibition and aspects of state control — was the invention in the 1950s of the continuous fermentation process by Morton Coutts. It was a world first, but more importantly for drinking Kiwis, it was better beer, and much more of it became available.

Most of the regional breweries have now closed and two major players, DB Breweries and Lion, dominate. There was a time when you

A Scandinavian picnic in Lowry Bay, 1896.

Vote 6 o'clock closing!

- IT MEANS FEWER BAD DEBTS —
- MORE MONEY FOR FAMILY COMFORTS —
- HAPPIER HOME LIFE

A poster depicting what a lovely home life we would have if six o'clock closing came into force, 1948.

could signal your arrival in Taranaki province by stopping off at the Awakino Tavern for a glass of Taranaki Ale, the locally made product. All around the country provincial breweries produced their own beer. Locals usually swore by it, and visitors often swore at it. The standard varied widely.

Kiwis, on their great 1950s pilgrimages through New Zealand, prided themselves on sampling the local beer of every province they entered and, eventually, left. Westbrew on the West Coast, Speight's in Otago and Waikato in the Waikato were just a sample of the regional beers tasted. Drinking beer on a wide geographical front was less controversial than the business of digging in at the local, to contribute to the six o'clock swill.

In 'polite' collections of Kiwiana, the six o'clock swill often misses out. Yet it was as Kiwi as corrugated iron. The national institution lasted for 50 years and helped give New Zealand an international reputation for primitive drinking habits. During World War I, it was spuriously decided to close the pubs at six o'clock, the better to preserve resources. Whether that was intended to mean that Kiwi males of war-serving age would be more sober when they were called up to become cannon fodder was questioned. The power of righteousness was identified as the real reason. Such interest groups often preferred total prohibition.

The six o'clock swill was not a pretty sight. Despite good womanly intentions, it became a male bastion. Women expected men to sip furtively and discuss the working day before heading home, agreeably affable and thirst-slaked. The reality was different. Pubs became swilleries. Men, often with a sense of defiance, did their best to down as much beer in the hour between knock-off time and the doom-laden call of 'Time, gentlemen, please'. Gentlemen? After sloshing away for an hour pub floors took the brunt. As much beer was spilt as was imbibed, some participants reckoned. The beer jug and seven-ounce glass held sway as thirsty, thwarted working men, out to prove that such strictures were unreasonable and unfair, produced an appalling cacophony. Legless wonders and drunken skunks eventually caught buses and trains (often going the wrong way), as the swill made its mark.

The six o'clock swill passed into antiquity in 1967 when ten o'clock closing was introduced, but Kiwis' binge drinking habits died hard. Indeed it has been postulated that teenage binge drinking of the new century owes something to the swill years.

The last day of the 'six o'clock swill' at the Porirua Tavern, October 1967.

'My Old Man's an All Black'

Rugby, race and beer

In a rugby-besotted land it is no surprise that one of the best remembered 'Kiwi' songs is 'My Old Man's an All Black', by the Howard Morrison Quartet.

At a time when local rock and pop music was caught between the early Elvis era and the emergence of the Beatles, the song made no pretence at being cutting edge. Indeed, it took the tune of Lonnie Donegan's British skiffle hit 'My Old Man's a Dustman', and with humorous local lyrics, largely by quartet member Gerry Merito, set about lampooning the situation of Maori exclusion from the 1960 All Blacks tour to South Africa.

At a time when the issue of such selection

The famous single was recorded at an actual performance at the Pukekohe Memorial Hall in 1960.

F (bar chords, or capo +3, play D, G, A)   Bb

policies had yet to engender social ferment among mainstream New Zealanders, the song generated a good-humoured, if perhaps naive, response. It summed up the political and social mindset of New Zealand in the early 1960s when a monocultural, Pakeha-dominated society not only allowed the All Blacks to tour apartheid South Africa without Maori representation, but could laugh about it as well.

The lyrics were written during a marathon car ride between Auckland and Wellington and back, in promoter Harry Miller's Jag. Howard Morrison's principal contribution to Merito's scribbles was the 'fe fi fo fum, there'r no horis in this scrum' aside.

The record of the song, which reputedly sold 60,000 copies, was based on a live recording laid down in the Pukekohe Town Hall while the Howard Morrison Quartet were undertaking one of their barnstorming tours of the country. Reports have it that the audience were locked in the hall until 1 am, until a suitably balanced reproduction of the song was achieved.

'My Old Man's an All Black' was redolent of a time in New Zealand's history — the last years of the post-war 'golden weather' of the 1950s and

early 60s, a period of prosperous innocence, soon to be shattered by more global issues like apartheid and civil rights. It was a brave person indeed who played the song during the tumult of the 1981 Springbok Tour.

THE HOWARD MORRISON QUARTET ON TV

The Howard Morrison Quartet featured on the cover of *Te Ao Hou* magazine in March 1962.

Sport & Entertainment

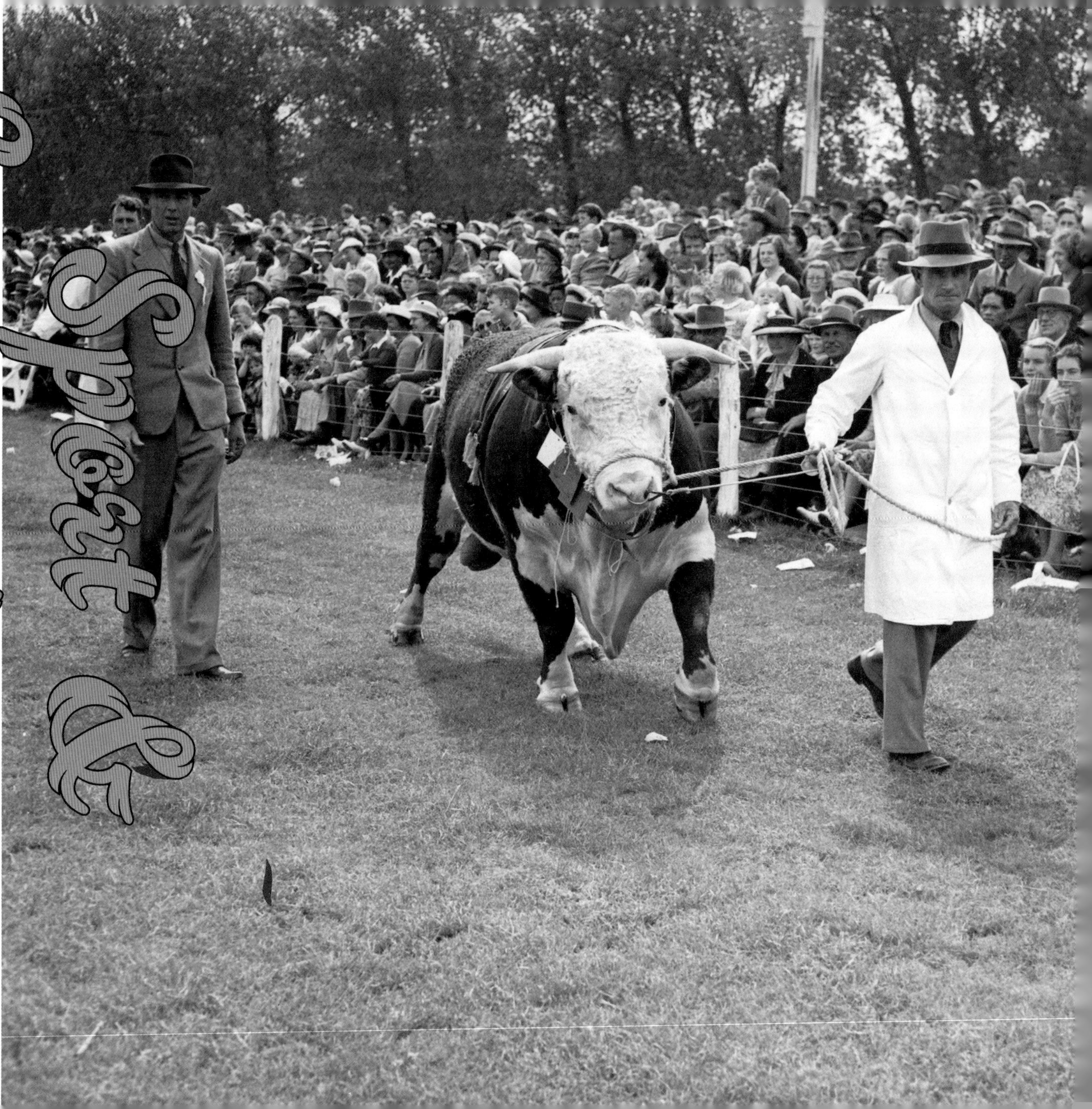

The A & P Show

Where work became sport

A distinctly New Zealand phenomenon, the A & P Show (agricultural and pastoral) was often a highlight of the summer, particularly in regions where farming and farmers were the 'backbone of the nation'.

Because of New Zealand's agricultural bounty such events had a certain inevitability. They were a formalised setting to see who had grown the largest pumpkin, or reared the best bull, pig or sheep. Equestrian events were a central feature but other agrarian-based activities like wood-chopping and sheep-shearing were tailored into meaningful competitions, where farmers did exactly what they normally did on the farm, only they did so while pitted against opponents and were able to come away with prizes for the fastest — and most efficient — efforts.

Mr Harry Barker's imported bull won first prize at the Gisborne A&P Show in July 1952.

Commentators figured it was odd that everyday farm tasks could be turned into 'virtual sports', but everyone, including the agricultural service town 'townies', loved it. Besides, there were also displays of shiny new tractors and trucks, and farming equipment — and then a grand parade of everything that moved. 'Townies' tended to look forward to the A & P Shows as much for the side-shows — the cluster of Ferris wheels, merry-go-rounds, dodgems, ghost trains and tent alleys of shooting ranges, hot-dog and candy-floss caravans, and chances to win fluffy animals of indeterminate genus by knocking down blocks with a wooden ball or dropping ping pong balls down the gob of some side-winding clown effigy heads. And, for all, there was highland dancing, as well as a beer tent usually located a safe distance from more wholesome activities.

Most Kiwis who can remember visiting the A & P Show in earlier times probably recall encounters with dodgy hot-dogs, often reheated to within an

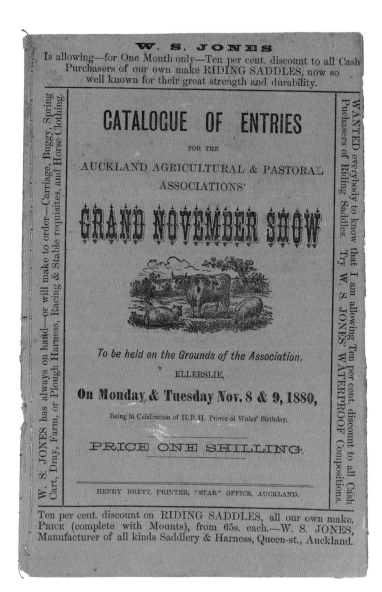

W. S. JONES
Is allowing—for One Month only—Ten per cent. discount to all Cash Purchasers of our own make RIDING SADDLES, now so well known for their great strength and durability.

W. S. JONES has always on hand—or will make to order—Carriage, Buggy, Spring Cart, Dray, Farm, or Plough Harness, Racing & Stable requisites, and Horse Clothing.

WANTED everybody to know that I am allowing Ten per cent. discount to all Cash Purchasers of Riding Saddles. Try W. S. JONES WATERPROOF Compositions.

CATALOGUE OF ENTRIES

FOR THE

AUCKLAND AGRICULTURAL & PASTORAL

ASSOCIATIONS'

GRAND NOVEMBER SHOW

To be held on the Grounds of the Association,

ELLERSLIE,

On Monday & Tuesday Nov. 8 & 9, 1880,

Being in Celebration of H.R.H. Prince of Wales' Birthday,

PRICE ONE SHILLING.

HENRY BRETT, PRINTER, "STAR" OFFICE, AUCKLAND.

Ten per cent. discount on RIDING SADDLES, all our own make. PRICE (complete with Mounts), from 65s. each.—W. S. JONES, Manufacturer of all kinds Saddlery & Harness, Queen-st., Auckland.

inch of their lives, and liberally daubed with enough tomato sauce to disguise any imperfections. It was all part of the fun of the fair and, anyway, standards have improved in recent years.

When steam was king and train travel at its peak, 'Show specials' were deployed to carry farmers and their families to A & P Shows. More than that, for many years the railway offered the only realistic means of getting livestock, produce and machinery to shows. Such was the significance of the shows that the government offered generous travel and haulage concessions on the rail excursions. The popularity of the A & P Show was reflected by the fact that in 1908 special trains carried 2000 Aucklanders to the Helensville Show.

The first A & P Associations were formed in the 1840s and by 1908 there were over 100 throughout New Zealand, each holding annual A & P Shows.

Many rural communities and some larger centres still hold shows. The 'Royal Show' tag is shared by the major A & P Associations and Show Day remains a public holiday in Canterbury.

The Catalogue of Entries for the Grand November Show, 1880.

Bungy Jumping

Leaping from great heights down under

Bungy jumping was based on the hair-raising practice of the Pentecost Islanders of Vanuatu, who were in the habit of tying vines around their ankles before diving off high wooden towers, secure in the knowledge that their plummet to certain death would be thwarted by the supporting vines.

That bungy jumping should take on iconic status in New Zealand was something of a surprise. Kiwis had always been regarded as cautious, careful, non-showy people. Our world renowned rugby was often conservative — until the time was right to cut loose. Better to keep your cards close and win by 3 than attempt a copy of Gaelic flair, and lose by 33. Our economy was similarly based on stolid, well-proven products of the land — something that Mother England wanted — rather than frivolous, speculative stuff.

Mind you, we had produced Sir Edmund Hillary the conqueror of Everest, and who would have bargained on a humble Kiwi beekeeper scaling such heights? Perhaps there's something in New Zealand's rugged, mountainous reaches that entices the likes of AJ Hackett to adapt the Pentecost Island habit of diving off high places and making little fanfare about it.

Hackett was the product of the 1980s when risks, mainly financial, were taken, as yuppie gurus, after the recession scares of earlier years, invited Kiwis to take the plunge, calculate their risk factors, feel the fear and do it anyway.

There were no wars to fight, yet male adrenalin and testosterone bubbled to the surface anyway. As a result adventure tourism developed, quite appropriately, in a country that was bursting with white water, black water, rugged hinterlands

and great heights. Older generations, seeking comfort after years of war and post-war rebellion, considered Hackett's endeavours to be mere show-off material, but soon bungy jumping became a Kiwi icon. Younger generations, hungry for adrenalin adventure, were diving off everything that didn't move. It wasn't hit or miss. Hackett, along with Henry van Asch, spent at least three years researching and refining the business of innocent travellers and tourists diving into the void with little more than elastic cords and ropes around their ankles. Kiwis were the guinea pigs, and nobody died, when New Zealand's first bungy jump was staged in 1988 at Queenstown.

Bungy jumping was then taken to the world. In 1987 Hackett himself had leapt off France's Eiffel Tower, which only encouraged more adventure tourists to travel to New Zealand to test their mettle on the new bungy jumping apparatus that was installed in some of the country's most scenic locations.

Straight down was not everyone's ideal way of seeing New Zealand, but for many young tourists it was a particularly Kiwi thing to do.

The face says it all. A terrifying piggy back bungy at AJ Hackett's.

Marching

Lifting spirits and hemlines

In the early 1960s young boys used to visit the local park of a Saturday morning to watch the teams of short-skirted marching teams go through their paces. The marching girls (there didn't appear to be any marching boys) provided a pubescent buzz in the years before that sort of action became more readily available in the emancipated days of the late 1960s.

Marching teams in New Zealand date back to the early days of the Great Depression. The Auckland YWCA fielded a team in 1931 and business houses like General Motors also entered combinations in provincial competitions. During the Depression years such teams marched at charity events, 'cheer-up' functions and fund-raising junkets. The marching routines, half sport, half performing arts, certainly raised the ardour of the males and the precision, sway and glamour of tightly choreographed routines took the women's minds off the hard times.

The New Zealand Marching Association was formed in 1945 and during World War II the various service corps provided inspiration in terms of uniforms and co-ordinated manoeuvres, many of them based on parade-ground

Leader Florrie McLeod and nine girls from the Sargettes marching team, 1951.

perambulations. Dressing up was part of the appeal for marching teams and soon midget and junior rankings were introduced, although it was still the seniors who held the line and attraction.

Marching reached its peak in the 1950s. By now marching teams punctuated pre-match and half-time brackets at major rugby games and other sporting events. In between times they contested regional and national championships, while glorying in names like Verdettes, and the more suburban-specific Remuera Guards. The latter with their tight-fitting, buttoned tunics and short, braided skirts rising several inches above the knee were a 1960s precursor to the mini skirt wearers who transformed the fashion landscape of the mid 60s. The social upheavals of the late 60s led to a more liberated, individualistic society where the regimentation, military-style uniforms and strict discipline of marching lost its appeal, as young women sought out alternatives.

In this day and age marching girls have given way to a more unstructured variant — the cheer-leaders and pre-match high-steppers who make many old-world, regimented marching girls cringe in their corporate boxes or wherever old marchers go.

Marching girls, the traditional variety, were a uniquely New Zealand phenomenon, despite their early association with US college drum majorettes. In their day they certainly raised the spirits.

Left: Marching girls await their turn at competition.

Horse Racing

Second leg of the rugby, racing and beer trifecta

Rugby, racing and beer were long regarded as the favoured activities of Kiwi blokes when they weren't raising kids, holding down a job and doing the lawns. All three icons have come under challenge in recent times from round-ball codes, casinos and wine, but certainly prior to the 1980s they were as Kiwi as, well, rugby, racing and beer.

Racing was deeply embedded in the national psyche. There were few boroughs and regions that didn't have their own racecourse during horse racing's pivotal years.

New Zealand's first known horse races involved the steeds of military garrisons during the days of the Land Wars. Anniversaries of the early European settlements were often marked by a celebratory race meeting. The century's first jockey club emerged in 1854 (the Canterbury Jockey Club). Three years later the first meeting of the Auckland Racing Club was staged.

New Zealanders took a particular shine to

Phar Lap winning his last race at Agua Caliente, Mexico, 1932.

horseracing. Many claimed they enjoyed the sight of well-trained horses stretching out along the home straight and the thrill of the chase. The chance to win a bob or two through betting was purely secondary, they claimed.

In a nation that commits more than a billion dollars to punting on the horses, the money aspect of horse racing may have been secondary, but it was a close second. As long ago as 1913 the world's first totalisator or 'tote' was set up at Ellerslie Racecourse. Invented by George Julius, an Australian, the new computer-like device took over from the many clerks required to operate the 'pari mutual' betting system formerly used on race tracks.

In 1921 bookmaking became illegal and in 1951 the Totalisator Agency Board or TAB opened betting shops to provide the convenience

A horse race on the West Coast.

of off-course betting. The TAB (or 'take a bet' as it was sometimes called) was established to stymie the often corrupt practices of off-course betting. By the early 1960s the TAB was the fifth most lucrative financial operation in New Zealand.

Kiwis continued to love a flutter on the horses and TAB turnover kept rising until the late 1980s when other fluttering options made their presence felt. Gaming machines, Lotto, Telebingo, Daily Keno, Instant Kiwi and casinos in general competed for the gambling dollar. The TAB countered with telephone betting, sports betting, and a more business-orientated approach.

Meanwhile, at grassroots level, the horses themselves have, over the years, developed iconic status. The famous Phar Lap, despite Australian's habit of claiming the champion as their own, was born in Timaru. Many remarkable Kiwi horses have excelled on the world stage. In 1983 perhaps the most symbolic — Kiwi — won the Melbourne Cup. In the same year Kiwi won the Japan Cup to present owner 'Snow' Lupton of Waverley with a double cause for celebration.

Sacha Olsen and Martyn Williams were runners up in the Cup Couture Fashion event during Auckland Cup Week, 2009.

'Now is the Hour'

A work still in progress?

It's a fair bet that most New Zealanders who know the song 'Now is the Hour' probably believe it is a traditional Maori melody. However, the origins of 'Now is the Hour' are traceable back to the 'Swiss Cradle Song', written by Clement Scott. It was first released in 1913 by WH Paling and Co., an Australian music company. Clement Scott was an Australian and his composition sold 130,000 copies. Not surprisingly, some of those copies ended up across the Tasman.

Around 1915 Maori words were added to the lilting tune, which was also changed slightly. As 'Po Atarau' it was sung as a farewell gesture to Maori soldiers departing for World War I. It was at this point that the belief arose surrounding its origins. It certainly sounded like a traditional Maori lament.

Maewa Kaihau provided further variation by writing an opening verse in English in 1920 that began, 'This is the hour'. She further modified the tune and added another Maori translation. Its popularity continued to grow and Maewa Kaihau claimed both the words and music as her work, although WH Paling and Co. insisted on the legitimacy of their ownership of the song's copyright. Despite that Kaihau's words were copyrighted.

To complicate matters further the first Maori words for the song were believed by some to have been the work of the Grace and Awatere families, sheep-shearers from Tuparoa.

The song was first recorded by Ana Hato in 1927. Hato, perhaps best known for her interpretation of 'Waiata Poi', written by Alfred Hill, began performing as a singer while still a child at her home-base, Whakarewarewa, Rotorua. Here she entertained tourists, many of whom were captivated by her treatment of 'Swiss Cradle Song' which had become 'Po Atarau'. Ana Hato's version, true to the song's lability, featured minor variations to the lyrics.

'Now is the hour/Po Atarau' continued to evolve. In 1935 Maewa Kaihau changed the title. Now as 'Haere Ra Waltz Song' it became popular as the last waltz at dances and other social functions and of course when soldiers were again farewelled to serve overseas in World War II.

After the war the song developed yet another life. In 1945 British songstress Gracie Fields visited New Zealand and heard the song performed by a Maori concert party in Rotorua. Gracie Fields' driver is credited with teaching the song to the spellbound singer who was so captivated by its haunting qualities that she expressed a desire to make a recording of her own. But not before further changes were made. Dorothy Stewart, Fields' manager, is credited with changing the opening line to 'Now is the Hour' and providing a further verse.

Eventually, in 1947, Gracie Fields sang her interpretation on BBC radio and when it was recorded 'Now is the Hour' became a massive world-wide hit, after occupying the number one position on English charts for 23 weeks. London Records, Gracie Fields' record company, were so enamoured of the catchy melody that they saw its American release as a chance to break into the lucrative USA market. A shipment of 24,000 copies, the largest consignment of a single record, was sent to Manhattan.

THE FAMOUS MAORI FAREWELL SONG AS FEATURED BY GRACIE FIELDS

NOW IS THE HOUR

(HAERE RA)

Words by
MAEWA KAIHAU

Music by
CLEMENT SCOTT

40c

Published in New Zealand by CHARLES BEGG & CO. LTD.
BY ARRANGEMENT WITH W. H. PALING & CO. LTD., SYDNEY
FOR SALE IN NEW ZEALAND ONLY

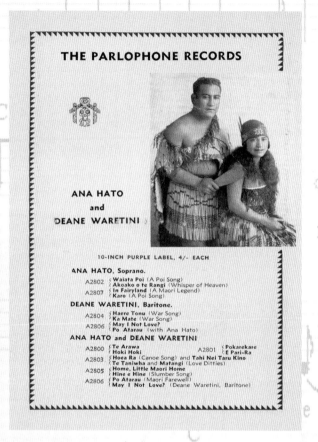

The song was soon scaling the USA charts.

It's hard to keep a good song down. It's just as hard to keep it to yourself. In early 1948 Bing Crosby released his version and it stormed to the top of the USA charts. Appropriately, it was Crosby's last single to reach number one in his home country.

Subsequently, Frank Sinatra, Kate Smith, Gale Storm and Eddy Howard all recorded versions of the song that 'everybody else was singing before Americans even heard of it'.

New Zealanders played a vital part in the song's evolution from Clement Scott's initial melody to the way it sounds today. It is now usually credited to Clement Scott, an Australian, Maewa Kaihau, a New Zealand Maori, and Dorothy Stewart, an Englishwoman.

A certain mystery surrounding its evolution remains, but one thing that seemed immutable was the tune's origins being the work of Clement Scott. Yet as long ago as 1948 there were counter claims over this apparent fact too. The widow of Albert Saunders claimed that her husband, a former worker at WH Paling and Co., had used the name 'Clement Scott' when selling his composition 'Swiss Cradle Song' to Palings in 1906. However, the manager of Palings, who was still alive at the time the claim was made, was adamant that Clement Scott was still alive too.

Irrespective of its origin, 'Now is the Hour' represents a fine example of the way Maori and European song traditions can blend together to produce a song that sounds intrinsically Kiwi.

Po atarau

(The 1915 version, sung to farewell Maori soldiers.)

Po atarau
E moea iho nei
E haere ana
Koe ki pāmamao

On a moonlit night
I see in a dream
You going away
To a distant land

Haere ra
Ka hoki mai ano
Ki i te tau
E tangi atu nei

Farewell,
But return again
To your loved one,
Weeping here

The Famous . .

Ana Hato
and the
TUHOURANGI
Maori Entertainers

will give their Unique Entertainment
in the

PEERLESS HALL
ROTORUA
Tuesday, Thursday and Saturday
at 8 p.m.

Price 3d.

ROTORUA PRESS

House & Garden

Quarter-acre Section

A little bit of land

As New Zealand was opened up for city, small town and suburban housing development, the quarter-acre section was factored into a residential landscape that always reflected New Zealanders' desire for space. With our low population density and surfeit of land the quarter-acre section was always a possiblility, one which satisfied the ideals of land ownership — one of the initial inducements to the early settlers.

Urbanisation was always set to be the next phase of human settlement in the new colony, yet rather than being constricted by land shortage, cities like Auckland championed the quarter-acre section, a factor that contributed to our major city's famous urban sprawl. There was no point building high-rise apartments when the land was available — and the Kiwi dream included ample lawns, room for gardens, sheds, orchards, chook runs, and later, swimming pools.

In a land of plenty of space the quarter-acre section meant that the backyard could accommodate a genuine 22-yard cricket pitch with provision for 10-yard bowlers' run-ups at either end, although it might mean angling your

Opposite: The kids play back yard tennis while the dads look on, 1925.
Above: 'The Section' circa 1911.

run-up to avoid colliding with the Hills Hoist clothesline or becoming garrotted on the cross-wires of an older lateral clothesline, or becoming ensnared in Mum's billowing rose blooms and thorns just before the point of delivery.

As houses bedded down and trees took root

on quarter-acre sections, tree huts for the kids appeared. Flying foxes were often erected. As life in New Zealand sped up, the quarter acre often assumed onerous maintenance obligations. Despite the egalitarian nature of society, New Zealanders and their quarter-acre paradises produced a few troubling eccentricities. One property owner concreted over his entire front lawn, although he compromised by painting it grass green. He decided he didn't have time to mow the frontage now that he was president of the local lawn bowls club — it being in the days when the six o'clock swill and commitments to home brewing in the back shed were also impacting.

Such eccentricities were in fact ahead of their time. In more recent years the cross-leasing phenomenon became common. Quarter-acre sections were carved up and Kiwis began living closer to one another. Much of the traditional Kiwi spirit of splendid isolation — even in the city — died. The notion of personal domain, where Kiwis could grow and cavort in comparative isolation, where there was room to swing several cats, gave way to smaller plots that, some say, has led to a heightening of neighbourhood tension.

As New Zealand became more urbanised, the quarter-acre section seemed an anachronism, although there were still many examples of the genre in smaller towns. Townhouses and high-rise apartments became common in the burgeoning cities as land became scarce and expensive.

It has been said that Kiwis became less homogeneous because of such developments. Without their quarter acres on which to express themselves, people became more withdrawn and exclusive, to the point where it became a popular dinner party utterance to say you hadn't seen your neighbours since last September. There was no longer any of that borrowing a cup of sugar over the back fence of the quarter-acre section, or communal working bees based on the concrete evidence of neighbourhood concrete mixers and subsequent bonding warm beer shouts sloshing from Crown Lynn tea cups.

Quarter-acre sections still exist of course, but they now represent a rather stately, less constricted Kiwi cornerstone. In the time-poor new century younger tenants no longer have the time to tend all that lawn, plant spuds, feed chooks and prune apple trees. And what's the point of borrowing a cup of sugar when you can visit the supermarket on your way to dine at the local café and spend most of your leisure time away from inner city flat, apartment or high-rise.

Kiwis no longer accept the right to a quarter-acre wedge of land as their birthright, preferring to adapt to high-rise apartment living or town-houses with a backyard that is often too constricted to even require a lawn mower.

Villas & Bungalows

Where we hung our hats

From the end of the nineteenth century until the years of World War I the bay villa was the most popular style of Kiwi home. Its origins are reasonably obscure, although some architects incline to the view that the idea came from the Bay area of San Francisco.

The villa was a considerable advance on the basic colonial cottage of earlier times in New Zealand. The latter was often only two-roomed, but as families continued to increase in size it was obvious that more room — and rooms — were required. It helped of course that New Zealand bristled with plentiful supplies of kauri, rimu, totara and matai timber.

Villas were essentially square with high ceilings (approximately three metres). From the outset they seemed eminently impractical. With New Zealand's often changing climate it was difficult to heat such waste space. They would have made more sense if the average height of the New Zealand adult was around eight feet tall, but rather than accept that local summers, although balmy, did not last all year, adaptations like fireplaces in living areas and bedrooms became a feature.

The interior layout of the villa was simple and orthodox (rather like its designers and occupants, someone suggested). A series of rooms opened out from each side of a large central hall. Service areas were located at the back of the house, down a central corridor.

If the basic structure was rudimentary the same could not be said of the villa's exterior. The front verandah was a feature. Its rails were moulded, timber adornments were fretted, as were the gables which were often surmounted by turned finials. The bay window (often two of them) was often an identifying protrusion.

While certain aspects of the villa were uncharacteristically flashy by New Zealand standards, it was reassuring to see the verandah used, not only for shelter, but for storage purposes. At the same time, though, it was interesting to contemplate the 'stylish' adornments like the verandah roof painted a different colour to the high, gabled main roof and leaded glass windows.

It was not surprising when the next 'new house on the block' presented, if nothing else, a pared back version of the more extreme and obvious bay villa features. Like its predecessor, the bungalow owed aspects of its origins to California, which had been influenced by Japanese architecture. While the villa was appropriate in terms of available materials and national aspirations, when the first of the Californian bungalows began sprouting, New Zealand was facing a time of war, austerity and a need to cut back, literally, on resources.

Not that the bungalow was pure California from the outset. Builders used the term to describe any detached dwelling that featured fewer of the villa's more prominent features. The most startling difference was the bungalow's lower roof. Fretwork and other frills were passed over. Double-hung sash windows were replaced

Villas overlooking Oriental Bay, Wellington.

by casement windows and leadlights.

The most revolutionary aspect of the new houses, apart from reducing all that wasted, aerial space, was a more flexible and commonsense use of floor area. Unlike the stoic aspect of the villa, which was always built to face the street, the bungalow's rooms were constructed to take advantage of the sun. And as New Zealand became less English and more egalitarian, kitchens and wash houses were designed to assist home owners and not 'household help'. The latter mindset had been the preserve of the villa and its builders and owners. But the bungalow still had its affectations for the affluent. Roughcast walls, exposed beams and contrasting timbers were regarded as decorative.

The distinctive bungalow round window.

The bungalow initially appeared in the first decade of the twentieth century and continued, until the late 1930s, to be the most popular style of house built in New Zealand. The Spanish mission style arrived in the 1920s, with its stucco, tiled roof and front porch.

The villa is still a dominant feature of the inner-city suburbs of our larger urban areas. Many years ago, the villa shared built-up areas with bungalows. The gentrification of the inner suburbs in recent decades for aesthetic and commuting purposes saved many of the old wooden wonders. Not only were they close to work but they took on a new charm for younger generations of home owners.

A lot of country kids in the 1960s encountered the villa for the first time. As university students or school leavers drawn to the cities they may have found themselves flatting in an old villa in an inner-city situation. Such old villas might have been cold and run-down, with the wind buckling the scrim walls and rattling the sash windows; the floors might have bucked and sloped, but there was plenty of space — and you could, if you had the wont, play indoor cricket in the generous central corridor. Rock music sounded better in the cavernous living areas and motor bikes and scooters fitted snugly in the front hall.

The villa suited communal living and mixed flatting as such lifestyle choices for young folk evolved, although it was hard to get that youth-flavoured cluttered look when furniture consisted of apple box seating, concrete-block book cases and beer-crate tables. The occasional table was 'occasional', although real, if partially disembowelled, sofas featured prominently on verandahs in living areas and even bathrooms.

The villa for such occupants was regarded as a castle. Freedom was asserted. It was better than living at home or in some closely chaperoned private boarding situation or institution — like student halls of residence. Besides, many young folk were now renouncing the materialism of their parents and the new little boxes made of ticky-tacky. The old villas were undergoing a resurgence.

Although many were bowled over, there came a time when inner-city villas became much sought after as 'do-uppers'. Young professionals now saw the potential in restoring the old houses. Gentrification of the tumble-down villas accelerated. Not only were the villas located conveniently close to the city, once renovated, they added a new charm. They scrubbed up well.

Masport Mower

Lawn order

New Zealand with its heritage of open spaces and long growing seasons, was always going to need something to keep the grass down around the house. Scythes were popular in early days. Tethered goats and free-range sheep were also popular means of preventing the fescues, browntop grasses, crested dogs-tail and cocksfoot from engulfing the home and making egress a difficult business. Clover and pesky paspalum were other obstacles.

In 1920 two New Zealand engineers, Reuben Porter and Harold Mason, created their own Auckland business, Mason & Porter. Twenty years later, as the problem of excessive grass growth around dwellings escalated, Mason and Porter produced a push mower called the Cleveland. The Masport (an obvious combination of Mason and Porter) Cleveland became a steel-bladed, low-cutting lawn mowing classic. You could even get a rubber-tyred version which reduced the clatter as it was trundled over concrete paths on a Sunday, when most lawn-mowing occurred.

As more Kiwis became house and property owners after World War II, the kitchen and house in general may have remained the preserve of the 'little woman', but the great quarter-acre outdoors was largely given over to the men. In earlier decades the trusty hand-mower, famous for snagging on clothes pegs, dropped kindling and un-tidied-away Buzzy Bees, basically kept the lawns in order. Inevitably, in an age when petrol-driven appliances developed credibility on the back of the burgeoning popularity of the motor car, motorised lawn mowers emerged. Often home-made, after hours of tinkering in the back shed, such devices were built to wartime, bomb-proof specifications and were difficult to push and manoeuvre. They were powerful machines. Buzzy Bees didn't stand a chance.

Often such heavy-duty monstrosities were activated in failing light by fathers and husbands who had arrived home from the pub and were last seen heading towards the chook run, pinpointed by the sparks given off as the mower glanced off concrete paths.

In 1952 an Australian named Mervyn Richardson produced the world's first rotary mower, the 'Victa'. Unlike the cylindrical mowers of old, the rotary version dealt to hardy lawn grasses like paspalum and were less cumbersome. The future of lawn mowers obviously belonged to the rotary mower and Masport developed the Rotacut rotary as a result.

These days the name 'Masport mower' is more readily associated with a rotary version, powered by a Briggs & Stratton engine, and

THE NEW SERIES

It's Easy with a **Masport**

RAPID BALL BEARING LAWN MOWER
MADE IN NEW ZEALAND

FAST CUTTING

The **Masport** LAWNMOWER

Masport New Zealand made Lawnmowers were first introduced to the market in 1930 and each successive year has seen large sales increases.

New Zealand labour and a considerable amount of local material is used in the production of this machine while the project is financed entirely by New Zealand Capital.

The five cylinder blades are of oil tempered and hardened Sheffield Steel. The British ball bearings require no adjustment after original fitting. Enclosed lubrication is embodied, and the whole machine is accurately fitted in every detail so that grass cannot penetrate to moving parts.

The Masport requires a minimum amount of effort to push and gives maximum cutting. Will cut very long grass and is adjustable at all essential points.

Sold by—

Opposite: The Masport 'Lawn Sprite', introduced in the 1950s.

Above: An advertisement for the new series Masport 'Rapid' which was introduced to the market in 1932.

pushed by fathers, mothers, sons and daughters, on any day of the week. Hand mowers like the Masport Cleveland have made a reappearance in these days of high petrol prices, noise abatement issues and a growing awareness of excessive carbon emissions and sedentary-job obesity.

Paua

The paua and the glory

Haliotis iris is not a strain of bad breath, nor does it have anything to do with the human eye. It is the most common form of New Zealand shellfish, of the abalone family, and can only be found in the sea around New Zealand. It is more readily known by the Maori name, paua, and is one of three species of the shellfish found in New Zealand waters.

While the dark-coloured meat of the paua is much sought after — producing a taste somewhere between steak and, not surprisingly, shellfish — it is the paua shell that has developed iconic status. The combination of blues, greens, purples and dabbles of pink on the inner shell were first appreciated by Maori who used them for decoration on carvings. Europeans found the shells just as alluring and they

Left: Paua shell jewellery is still popular today.

soon became utilised for souvenirs, jewellery and fishing lures. The iridescent surface can be traced to the paua's feeding habits, with those that target brown kelp as their principal food source producing the attractive hues.

In earlier days paua shells were used as ashtrays. But with folk these days having a greater respect for the paua, not to mention there being far fewer smokers, the paua shell ashtray is seen no more.

Ironically, the outer shell of the paua provides its survival mechanism. It is as dull and nondescript as the inner shell is brilliantly iridescent. For this reason paua are easily overlooked on the sea bed or rocks at a depth between one and 10 metres. The paua shell does not give up its eye-catching bounty easily and the encrusted sea growth must be ground away to reveal the beauty beneath.

Such is the iconic status of the paua shell that a Southland couple, Fred and Myrtle Flutey, decorated their Bluff home with shells in general and paua shells in particular. The living-room walls

of the nationally known Paua Shell House were covered with whole paua shells from local beaches. In recent times, amid controversy, the Paua Shell House collection was relocated to Canterbury Museum. Myrtle and Fred passed away in 2000 and 2001 respectively, but their legacy and that of the paua lives on.

Crown Lynn

No-nonsense receptacles from a respected pottery

Pat. No. 428

Mogambo

COOK & SERVE

by Crown Lynn

NEW ZEALAND

The company that made the railways cup, out of which thousands of New Zealanders supped many gallons of tea and coffee while travelling on passenger trains of old, was originally formed to manufacture sewer pipes, among other things. The Amalgamated Brick & Tile Company of Auckland, formed in 1929, expanded its production during World War II as a result of wartime crockery shortages. Formerly crockery had been imported but, as a luxury item, it was now time for a local manufacturer to stand up. The Amalgamated Brick & Tile Company formed a Specials Department to undertake work, including crockery, that was outside its standard range.

One of its first major assignments was to make crockery for the American Navy. Then, in 1943, came the epochal call from New Zealand Railways for a rugged cup suitable for use on passenger trains. It didn't seem like it at the time but the eventual outcome was an item that would develop iconic status and become a standard Kiwiana item. It certainly didn't seem like it when the first version of the cup came incomplete, without handles. After much jostling and slopping and burnt fingers as train passengers negotiated their way back into swaying carriages, a handle became a necessary adjunct.

After the war the Specials Department of the Amalgamated Brick & Tile Company morphed into a separate body — Crown Lynn — in 1948. It was located in the Auckland suburb of New Lynn and its name was believed to owe something to its location. Crown Lynn specialised in domestic and art crockery, and vitrified hotelware, and went on to become a market leader in these items. Kiwi and swan vases were among its most popular wares and many of these graced the mantelpieces of Kiwi homes. Just as significantly, Crown Lynn developed a range of crockery that owed less to the cluttered style of English potteries and more to a pragmatic, simple Kiwi design. No item represented this development better that the railways cup.

'Mogambo' was the design of one of Crown Lynn's first 'coffee cans'.

Crown Lynn became so popular that by 1959 they were able to celebrate the one-hundred-millionth item of pottery to pass through their portals. The following year close to 10,000,000 pieces were produced in what was now the largest

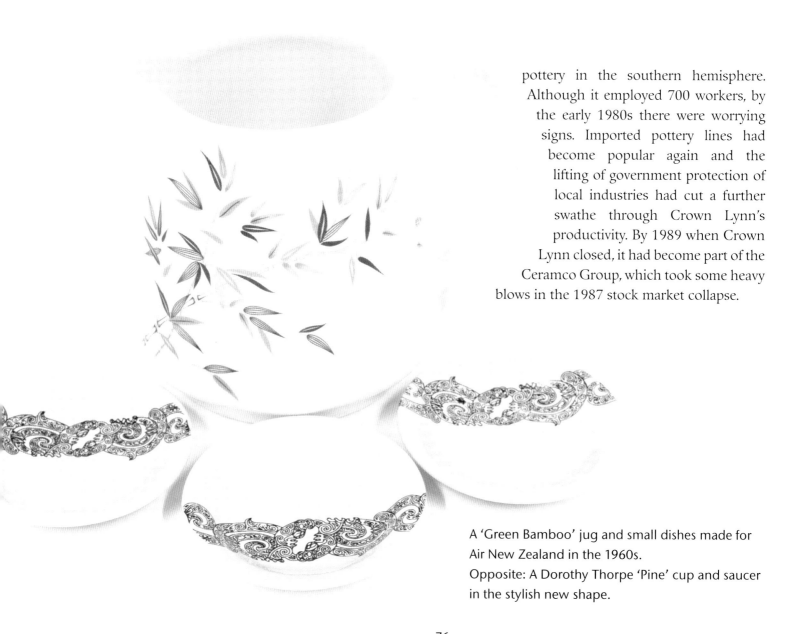

pottery in the southern hemisphere. Although it employed 700 workers, by the early 1980s there were worrying signs. Imported pottery lines had become popular again and the lifting of government protection of local industries had cut a further swathe through Crown Lynn's productivity. By 1989 when Crown Lynn closed, it had become part of the Ceramco Group, which took some heavy blows in the 1987 stock market collapse.

A 'Green Bamboo' jug and small dishes made for Air New Zealand in the 1960s.
Opposite: A Dorothy Thorpe 'Pine' cup and saucer in the stylish new shape.

Of course, the need for railways cups had ceased many years earlier when railway refreshment rooms closed down, but that didn't diminish the memories. The railways cup was built to last. Some wag suggested they were so rock-like, they could derail a large steam engine if left on the line. They certainly could chip your teeth in a one-on-one with enamel, as the train bucked and swayed. They were robust enough to survive rough handling by train guards as they collected and corralled them in wire baskets and kerosene-tin containers from carriage floors.

They were seasonal too. In the rugby season drunken rugby fans used to kick and bounce them along station platforms in impromptu games, on the way back from the test match. In the cricket season they were used as balls by drunken cricket fans as they re-enacted test match events at Eden Park earlier in the day. If you were lucky you could get them to bounce like a Richard Hadlee delivery or turn like an Indian spinner's leg break.

Obviously, there were casualties and broken cups often littered the trackside, were cast off viaducts or were swallowed up by the Wangamarino Swamp. These days they are highly sought after collectibles but in the heyday of rail travel they were eminently expendable.

Edmonds Cookery Book

Of tripe and suet pudding

Edmonds Cookery Book was born out of Thomas Edmonds' desire to make and distribute his own brand of baking powder to boost trade in his Lyttelton grocery. In 1879 Edmonds also coined the famous 'sure to rise' slogan, based on verbal assurances he gave to a customer when the latter asked if the new baking powder would actually work. Eventually, Edmonds constructed

a landmark factory and the Edmonds brand became a national favourite. The baking powder became a Kiwi staple and by 1928, 2.5 million tins were being sold annually.

When the *Edmonds Cookery Book* was published it contained recipes that, not surprisingly, stipulated the need for Edmonds' baking powder. It was a brilliant piece of 'parallel marketing'. Indeed the first edition was little more than a promotional tool for the baking powder. For some time it was free and targeted at engaged couples.

Kiwis love reading books. They also like food. Predictably, five of New Zealand's all-time best-selling books have been cooking-related. The *Edmonds Cookery Book*, apart from the Bible, has been New Zealand's best selling book ever. Between

Left: The famous Edmonds factory.
Opposite: Four editions of the *Edmonds Cookery Book* — 1st, 4th, 6th and the 16th Deluxe edition.

1908 and 1955 it was released in its economy edition. The deluxe version has been published since 1955. By 2001 it had sold 3.5 million copies.

That the book boasted the claim of containing economical everyday recipes was evidenced by the inclusion during certain eras of Good Plain Cake, Mashed Potatoes, and Tripe and Suet Pudding. It has been regularly updated, although Tripe and Suet Pudding no longer features.

All that is left of the original Edmonds factory is a garden enclosure in Christchurch. Goodman Fielder now own the brand. But the ever-popular cookery book remains, with the front cover showing the old factory in Ferry Road, as a reminder of the source of Edmonds Baking Powder. The factory has long gone but the book continues to thrive as it heads beyond 100 years of publication.

Yates Garden Guide

Green thumb bible

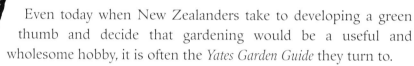

Even today when New Zealanders take to developing a green thumb and decide that gardening would be a useful and wholesome hobby, it is often the *Yates Garden Guide* they turn to.

Our moist, temperate climate means that growing conditions for vegetables, flowers, shrubs and trees (and lawns and weeds) are ideal and our access to tracts of suitable growing land, particularly when the quarter-acre section was a standard concomitant of home ownership, means that gardening in general has often been a feature of New Zealand life.

Arthur Yates, the founder of what is now known as Yates NZ Ltd, arrived in New Zealand in 1879. His family back in England had been seed merchants in Manchester and after working initially on New Zealand farms, Yates sensed an opening for a local seed merchant organisation. Arthur Yates and Company was the upshot, founded in Auckland in 1883. Such was the success and growth of the company that, by 1911, a six-storey head office, housing warehouse, retail facility, plant nursery, packing plant and seed-cleaning section had been opened in Albert Street, Auckland.

Yates seeds became a cornerstone of the New Zealand lifestyle. Vegetables for him, flowers for her, although such generalisations often overlooked the contribution made by mothers-at-home to the burgeoning cabbage patches and silver beet plots. In hard times the home vegetable garden supplemented the family income and diet. In harder times, like the Great Depression, the products of vege gardens represented the difference between a family going hungry or not. And the wholesomeness of the home-grown potatoes, tomatoes, cauliflower, cabbage, silver beet, onions, carrots, leeks and other vegetables, which began life as Yates seeds, enhanced the respectability of the exercise.

It was not surprising that an instructional gardening publication should become an icon of this most Kiwi of passions. The *Yates Garden Guide* was first published back in 1895 and such has been its popularity that it has sold over 7 million copies and over 70 editions.

Despite the decline of gardening in recent years because of factors like urbanisation, cross-leasing and eating out, it's amazing how many copies of the *Yates Garden Guide* can be found in garage, back shed or book case, even in homes where books are not a dominant item. In the last a handful of Barry Crump yarn collections, a few rugby biographies and the *Edmonds Cookery Book* will invariably be represented — and the *Yates Garden Guide*.

The 41st (1961) edition of the *Yates Garden Guide*.

Garden Ornaments

Making a statement

At a time in the 1950s and 1960s when suburbs burgeoned and new houses and recently sowed sections encroached on former farm land, butterflies and garden gnomes, as adornments to the quarter-acre section, and the house itself, were common.

The butterfly emerged in the 50s. Made of cut-out metal as multi-coloured adornments to weatherboard homes — facing the road, of course, because everyone needed to see them — butterflies on houses were often regarded as more kitsch than Kiwiana. Perhaps cut-out Kiwis or profiles of All Blacks may have made more sense, or even a likeness of Michael Joseph Savage, portraits of whom adorned the mantelpiece of many pro-Labour Kiwis at the time. Metal butterflies on houses were often a source of embarrassment to non-approving kin, but you can still see them today, rusting in the suburbs, redolent of a less complex time.

Perhaps the butterflies were seen as necessary to break up the monotony of the new, standardised post-war weatherboard house. Certainly, as part of the Sunday drive around the new sub-divisions, the kids in the back seat could be deflected from mischief by counting the number of butterflies along the route. It was a bit like seeking out white horses during the course of drives into the country.

Garden gnomes, made from concrete moulds, were another adornment that made little sense, artistically or otherwise, although until would-be burglars got used to them, they seemed to serve as big-eyed, if stationary, watch-dogs.

Old bike frames draped with creepers, car tyres sprouting rhododendrons and carefully placed car mudguards, mounted with morning glory, were some of the adornments found in suburban front yards.

In a time of extreme conservatism such embellishments were seen to represent Kiwis making personal statements. Of course, the discarded car bodies on some front lawns tended to make statements of another kind.

Rinso, Handy Andy and Janola

'Keep it clean'

The 1918 flu epidemic that accounted for around 8600 New Zealand deaths forced citizens to take issues of hygiene and health seriously. The development of household cleansers took on a new urgency. Carbolic, pumice and imported disinfectants like 'Kerol', which apparently 'kept plague away', became popular. The development of laundry soap, the precursor to Rinso, had seen the development of the Taniwha brand and Lever's Sunlight Soap. The latter came in distinctive yellow bars and looked like blocks of hard cheese.

Not long after Sunlight's introduction a workman at a New Zealand railway station, taking advantage of the new soap's likeness to cheese, filled his lunch-time sandwiches with slices of Sunlight soap. One of the workman's colleagues had been in the habit of helping himself to the workman's cheese sandwiches without invitation. Now, as the colleague munched eagerly into his ill-gotten gains, and foam began bubbling at the corners of his mouth, no one said a word. To his credit the colleague finished the Sunlight sandwiches before retreating to lick his wounds. There was no more pilfering of someone else's cheese sandwiches, not at that particular railway station anyway.

Rinso became a household name after Selwyn Toogood, host of several popular radio programmes, plugged the product. Rinso and Lux, a flaky laundry soap, were first produced at Lever's new flake mill in Petone in 1924 and, until the advent of automatic washing machines, were the housewife's first line of defence against dirty laundry.

While Lever products predominated it was Reckitt and Colman who came up with an all-purpose cleanser that now enjoys the status of household name. Janola was the concoction produced by two Auckland manufacturers. The name derived from a combination of the Christian names of their wives, Jan and Nola.

In 1959 Lever brothers first produced Handy Andy which, like Janola and Rinso, became a Kiwi icon. Handy Andy, a cleanser with a boy's name, effectively took over from Clever Mary, an earlier product that held sway from the 1920s to the 1950s. Cynics could suggest that Handy Andy might have met opposition as a trade-name, particularly as it was essentially women who used it. Back in the 1960s many women warmed to the name. It was like having a man about the house to help with onerous chores in the years

before sharing of household cleaning duties became common.

In 1982 Rinso was withdrawn from the market and Persil, a product capable of releasing bleach, took centre stage on washing day. Janola and Handy Andy continue the battle against grime.

The Bloke's Shed

Atoms split for free

When men came in from the border, where they had been in early aeons, protecting women and children from raiding warriors, and herds of wild beasts, they had to go somewhere. The industrial revolution and urbanisation reduced the wandering, nomadic, food gathering ways of males and based them close at hand to the steel mills, factories and ship-building yards they now patrolled. But men still needed a place to retreat to, be it pub, street corner or outside shed.

In New Zealand, once urbanisation took flight, the quarter-acre section reduced man's bordering propensities and a sense of confinement set in. Soon the bloke's shed became as integral a part of the quarter-acre landscape as the barbecue and cluster of concrete gnomes in the front garden. The male of the Kiwi species needed his own space, and a place to potter and ponder.

The bloke's shed was traditionally the tool shed. The humble lean-to or more upright affair housed lawnmowers, spades, ladders and car-parts, and doubled as a storeroom for the daughter's furniture while she decided whether to move into a flat with her boyfriend. It was a great place to store the items that would 'come in handy one day'. Then it became a repository for home-brew manufacture, a strange-smelling environment where brown brews gurgled and bottle tops occasionally exploded into the ceiling.

Blokes' sheds often contained 'beer fridges', radios and later small TV sets, the better to listen to or watch the big games, where a handful of locals could cluster to cheer on the favourites, sample a brew or two, yell and curse with impunity well away from the family hearth and the kid's ears.

Given Kiwis' propensity to invent, it was no surprise that the bloke's shed was often given over to tinkering with mechanical bits and pieces.

Sacred duties like realigning the transverse flange on the reverse mechanism of the standard organ-grinder took place in the shed. Cars were repaired, stripped or even built from scratch.

Kiwi ingenuity, as it applied to blokes, was often best expressed in the bloke's shed, and a best-selling book called *Blokes & Sheds*, published in 1998, championed the cause of many shedsters and their dwellings in some depth and with much sincerity. One suspects that Jim Hopkins, the book's author, may have written parts of the manuscript in the shed.

Often blokes' sheds doubled as half-way houses. When mates were banished from the house by the wife, a bed of sorts was always available 'out the back' in Bill's shed. Lumpen and lumpy it might have been, but it was a place to lay your weary head. In other ways, access to blokes' sheds has provided companionship for males, succour, food (baked beans on the primus), beer (homebrew from the 'gurgler' or real beer from the 'beer fridge') and acceptance (you could stay all night but had to patch things up with Ngaire before the missus found out).

Rotary Clothesline

What goes around comes around

During the house-building boom of the 1950s and 1960s, there was always a revolving, upright clothesline standing starkly out the back of the quarter-acre section. In earlier times linear clothes lines often linked from tree to tree, fence to tree or house to outhouse, sagged with loads of dripping, drying washing supported by wooden poles that kids playing 'chasey' would often dislodge, leaving garments dangling in the dirt. Furthermore, kids — and grown-ups too — were prone to render themselves almost garrotted as they failed to see the line on non-washing days, and gentlemen's hats were knocked off in embarrassing fashion. While such a device would serve as an effective anti-burglar device in this day and age, back then traditional clotheslines could be a curse.

Flax was a popular raw material for very early clotheslines before galvanised wire came along — despite its propensity to rust and leave red-brown smudges on sheets and smalls. Then an Australian named Lance Hill appeared to have solved the problem of the linear clothesline by producing, in the 1940s, the first rotary clothesline, based on an upright steel strut — the 'single steel tree' it was sometimes referred to — which was far more compact and user-friendly.

Housewives could now twirl the new rotary clothesline (the Hills Hoist), which despite its compactness still provided over 100 feet of pegging space. There was no longer any need to wallow through often soggy underfoot New Zealand conditions while hanging out the washing.

While the Hills Hoist bedded in as a standard adjunct to the 50s and 60s quarter-acre section, it attracted attention for some of the wrong reasons. Husbands who dabbled in duck shooting were prone to hang pre-plucked birds on the new clothesline, away from scavenging dogs. Wives resented having to share the clothesline with such macabre offerings. Kids too used the Hills Hoist for functions not included in accompanying brochures. Mum's new clothesline was a dead-ringer for the merry-go-rounds ridden at A & P shows and some inventive kids attached wooden box seats to the line with No. 8 wire hooks and charged their mates sixpence to ride on the sagging and often compromised rotary clothesline.

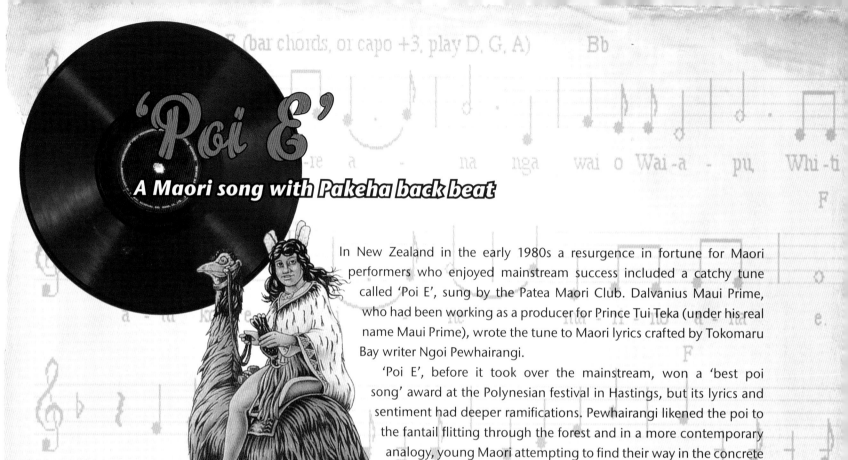

'Poi E'

A Maori song with Pakeha back beat

In New Zealand in the early 1980s a resurgence in fortune for Maori performers who enjoyed mainstream success included a catchy tune called 'Poi E', sung by the Patea Maori Club. Dalvanius Maui Prime, who had been working as a producer for Prince Tui Teka (under his real name Maui Prime), wrote the tune to Maori lyrics crafted by Tokomaru Bay writer Ngoi Pewhairangi.

'Poi E', before it took over the mainstream, won a 'best poi song' award at the Polynesian festival in Hastings, but its lyrics and sentiment had deeper ramifications. Pewhairangi likened the poi to the fantail flitting through the forest and in a more contemporary analogy, young Maori attempting to find their way in the concrete Pakeha jungles. Such urban drift was made more poignant by the closure of the Patea freezing works, forcing many young Maori to leave town in search of work. 'Poi E' had a political point to make as well as becoming a Kiwi party favourite and a number one hit in 1984.

Dalvanius, in seeking singers of the song, looked no further than the local Maori Club in his home town, Patea. It was a masterstroke. The South Taranaki Cultural Club had been formed in the 1970s, a small town Maori chorale traditionally called upon to sing at civic celebrations and marae welcomings. Renamed the Patea Maori Club, Dalvanius unleashed them at Mascot Studios where their enthusiastic vocals were complemented by an Auckland-based rhythm section that included Tama Renata, Stuart Pearce and Alastair Riddell. The combination of traditional Maori vocalisations and a funky instrumental backing produced a sound that appeared initially to be irresistible.

Dalvanius also had his own record label, Maui, and in 1983 'Poi E' was released on Maui to encouraging reviews. It screened on TV on *Radio with Pictures* and *Ready to Roll*.

1983 was also the year when New Zealand's break-dancing phenomenon reached its zenith. Bop-dancing teams strutted their stuff all over the place, although Aotea Square was a leading squaring off location. Break-dancing was a predominantly Polynesian pastime and the link with 'Poi E', as a break-dancing accompaniment, was not surprising

when the break-dancing kids lent a keener ear to the Patea Maori Club's song.

Early in 1984 TV led to the song's elevation. *Eye Witness News*, though more concentrated on the news component of the break-dancing culture than the musical impetus, indirectly provided the exposure for 'Poi E' which, still without much in the way of radio backing, scaled the New Zealand hit parade to reach number one in March. It remained there for four weeks.

'Poi E' struck such a chord that it spawned an album in 1996 and an earlier rock musical which was staged in New York and London and was afforded a royal command performance in Edinburgh, Scotland.

In 2010, 'Poi E' is once again again popular due to its inclusion in Taika Waititi's box-office hit 'Boy'.

But back in the early 1980s, when issues of racism and Maori rights came to the fore, 'Poi E' was a rallying song for both Maori and Pakeha.

Poi E

TE POI!
PATUA TAKU POI PATUA KIA RITE
PA-PARA PATUA TAKU POI E!

E rere ra e taku poi poro-titi
Ti-taha-taha ra whaka-raru-raru e
Poro-taka taka ra poro hurihuri mai
Rite tonu ki te ti-wai-waka e

Ka pare pare ra pi-o-o-i-o-i a
Whaka-heke-heke e ki a kori kori e
Piki whaka-runga ra ma mui-nga mai a
Taku poi poro-titi taku poi e

CHORUS
Poi E whaka-tata mai
Poi E kaua he rereke
Poi E kia piri mai ki au
Poi E-E awhi mai ra
Poi E tapeka tia mai
Poi E o taua aroha
Poi E pai here tia ra
POI . . . TAKU POI E!

RERE ATU TAKU POI TI TA' TAHA RA
WHAKARUNGA WHAKARARO TAKU POI E!

Clothing

Swanndri

How to keep your swan dry, if you have one

The swanndri, a hooded, knee-length, all-wool outdoor garment, was tailor-made for New Zealand's rugged lifestyle and climatic conditions. The man concerned in the original creation of the iconic bushshirt was William Broome of Taranaki who patented the first swanndri in 1914. Broome, a clothing manufacturer, had introduced the swan trademark and in attempting to concoct a name that incorporated both the swan label and the distinctive waterproof qualities of the new 100 percent woollen garment, produced a strange hybrid — swanndri. 'Swan dry' became 'Swanndri'. The addition of an extra 'n' was something of a mystery, as was the use of 'dri' instead of 'dry'.

The double 'n' and 'i' on the end lent a foreign tone and appearance to the term. Some believed that swanndri was an Indian word, in a similar vein to Indian derivatives like 'dinghy', although the latter ended in 'y'. Others reckoned swanndri derived from Italian, although Italy's Mediterranean climate would scarcely have necessitated a garment — and word — that reflected Italian conditions. Such a realisation diminished the Indian claim too.

In 1937, John McKendrick of New Plymouth bought the Swanndri trademark and business. He modified the famous bush shirt by adding sleeves and a hood, and by making them out of pre-shrunk fabric.

Over the years the word swanndri was shortened affectionately to 'swanny', such was its preponderance and popularity as New Zealand's favourite outdoor shirt. The swanndri itself, after starting out as exclusively green in colour, expanded to encompass different patterns and colours. Soon, not only did farmers swear by them, but bushmen, army personnel and fishermen appreciated their warmth and water resistance, the latter a result of the pre-shrinking process that improved their water resistance. The swanndri, in combination with balaclava, gumboots and denim jeans, became the complete look for the great Kiwi outdoors.

Once exclusively rural, the swanndri was taken up by city dwellers in more recent times and when the tourism industry boomed it was ideal for adventure tourists as they tramped through New Zealand's famous terrain and changeable showery weather.

From humble beginnings the swanndri has spawned a collection of leisure jackets and shirts that have become known around the world. In terms of leisure the swanndri itself has become a favourite of young party-goers, particularly students from Dunedin, where the winter's bite and pub crawling demands a step out into the great outdoors between taverns.

Jandals

Sandals with a 'J'

Before jandals there were sandals — Roman, with complex leather cross wrungs and hard soles that often came adrift after much wear and tear, and often got stuck in the tar of melted mid-summer asphalt pavements. Some sandals were simply abandoned in the tar as the relentless January sun beat down.

When jandals came along in the late 50s, they were regarded as the greatest thing since sliced bread. You didn't even have to bend down to don them. Their rubbery presence provided reasonable comfort and once you got used to the gap between the big toe and the next one along as the securing mechanism, you barely noticed the revolutionary intrusion.

The jandal owes its name to one Maurice Yock who, while travelling through Asia, picked up on local footwear known in other parts of the world as 'flip-flops' and 'thongs'. Yock worked for J. Yock & Company, his grandfather's shoe manufacturing concern, and when he returned to Auckland and helped set up mass manufacture of 'Japanese sandals', the brand name Jandal struck a chord. 'Jandals Ltd' produced the pivotal summer footwear, initially in a Te Papapa garage. Such was the popularity of the new footwear that

96

Skellerup eventually bought out the operation.

Before too long thousands of Kiwis were wearing jandals. They were a killingly simple adaptation, although even today they are regarded as somewhat crude attire, and wearers are not permitted entrance to certain functions and establishments. Roman sandals, meanwhile, have retained a certain respectability.

New Zealand kids have gone from the barefoot look (even in winter many defied the frost and frozen puddles with thick-skinned indifference), through structured boots at a time when society regarded solid footwear as being essential to support growing ankles, to the contemporary situation where casual footwear (including jandals) is regarded as the norm.

Gumboots

'If it weren't for your gumboots'

Since 1943 when Skellerup produced their first rubber gumboots called Marathon, New Zealand has led the world in gumboots manufacture. In 1958 with the release of Skellerup's Red Band model, a mid-calf adaptation, not only Kiwi farmers but backyard gardeners and sports spectators became avid wearers of a product that defied New Zealand's often wet and clinging underfoot conditions.

Comedian Fred Dagg popularised the gumboot in the 1970s. Indeed his most popular song eulogised the waterproof icon. 'If it weren't for your gumboots where would you be? . . .'. Several years later the small town of Taihape, seeking an identity and re-branding following the decline of farming and the railways, came up with an annual gumboot-throwing competition, an event that attracts a large following and a

A man, his dog and his gumboots.

significant number of tourists and their dollars.

Most Kiwis have memories of wearing gumboots. Rural back porches are usually adorned with mud-splattered examples (you're not allowed to wear them indoors) and more and more urban dwellers are appreciating their practicality and ease of application (you can virtually walk into them).

With the encroachment of global warming and changing weather patterns, leading to increased rainfall and outdoor pugginess in some urban areas, it is not unreasonable to suggest that gumboots could gain a foothold, not only as a practical counter to street puddles, overflowing stormwater drains and yielding if tiny backyards, but as a fashion accessory. Already the 'bikini and gumboots' combo has emerged down on the farm and at the beach in the humid heat of summer, and as a further adaptation to our warming land, more than one streaker has punctuated proceedings in cricket test matches, as rain stopped play, by invading the pitch wearing nothing but sun hat and gumboots.

Walk shorts and Stubbies

Walk this way — and that

Walk shorts were regarded as somehow liberating for men, when they first appeared as a fashion item in the 1960s. At a time when the mini skirt proved so revolutionary for women, with hemlines marching triumphantly above the knee, the blokes now saw some glory in flashing their knees as well, just to prove that the seeds of 60s revolution had been sown in their direction too.

It helped if you had reasonable legs, just like the unspoken stricture of mini skirt use. The knobbly-kneed, bandy-legged, chicken-spoked and salami-calfed were often the subject of ridicule as they strutted, loped and galumphed around the workplace. It didn't help that walk shorts in the workplace were sanctioned and sometimes expected, but only if they were accompanied by white shirt (tie optional), sensible, restrained bland shoes (black or perhaps brown) and non-floppy socks that at least preserved a modicum of leg coverage.

The shorts themselves had to be of a superior cut — like shortened longs — with appropriate creases and pockets. They were in fact truncated trousers.

They were particularly comfortable at the height of summer, in days before air-conditioning came along. And walk short wearers seemed more approachable. A car salesman, bank manager, or public servant who wore walk shorts often presented as being more jovial, generous and trustworthy. Perhaps it was the subconscious notion that if he'd gone to the trouble of showing us his knees, he would be less inclined to rip us off or turn down our application for a bank loan.

Walk shorts were far more accommodating than another development in men's accoutrements: Stubbies. These were essentially tight, recreational shorts for males, which evolved on the back of walk shorts. Although they were first established in 1972 by Edward Fletcher & Co, an Australian company, Kiwi males strutted around in them as if they were our own invention.

Again, after the mini skirt, it was now time for New Zealand males to show off certain attributes. Stubbies may have represented part of male emancipation, the way the mini had for females, but they were similarly challenging for the wearer. They had tight elastic waists, and very little room in the buttock region. They were so constricting that Kiwi males didn't so much strut their stuff as effect a stiff-legged waddle. The bum crack broke new ground too as a male fashion statement.

Beige was a popular colour, but brave browns and dark blue and black versions of the cotton-polyester garment were not unknown. Extra features included a small key pocket with a flap at the front and a back pocket, access to which was almost impossible because of the constricting nature of the shorts.

Stubbies followed walk shorts into antiquity in the 1980s. It was the end of an era. References to Stubbies can still be found, however, in the form of historical flash-backs. A down-under dictionary lists and defines Stubbies as 'Short shorts of tough material for informal wear'. You had to be tough to wear them too.

'Pokarekare Ana'

New Zealand's unofficial national anthem

Many New Zealanders grew up with 'Pokarekare Ana', a traditional Maori love song. When increasing numbers of Kiwis found themselves overseas, either in time of war or on OE, and a 'song of home' was called for in social settings, many fell back on 'Pokarekare Ana'.

There have been many claims relating to the song's origins. An East Coast Maori song-writer, Paraire Henare Tomoana was reputed to have penned the song in 1912 in the interests of winning the heart of Kuini Repeka Ryland while performing the song at a Gisborne marae. Tomoana, who refined the song in 1917 and published the words in 1921, claimed that it originated from north of Auckland.

Another view is that Sir Apirana Ngata wrote the song while another is that Sir Apirana and Tomoana composed it together. The actions illustrating the song were believed by some to have been added by Sir Apirana Ngata in 1917.

Although such issues have never been resolved, guardianship of the words and music are held by the family and descendants of Paraire Tomoana, although it is generally regarded as being communally composed.

The Maori words have remained basically unchanged over the years, but many different English translations have emerged. Just as many recording artists around the globe have performed and recorded the song, including Prince Tui Teka, Dame Malvina Major, a British classical group called Angelis and more recently (in 2003), Hayley Westenra on her best-selling *Pure* album. Perhaps the best-known version was that of Dame Kiri Te Kanawa.

'Pokarekare Ana' has wartime associations. It emerged in its refined form during the years of World War I and was popularised by Maori soldiers while they were training near Auckland, before leaving to fight in Europe. During the Korean War in the early 1950s Kiwi soldiers taught the tune to Korean children. The song is still sung by the people of South Korea.

Close to home 'Pokarekare Ana' is sometimes regarded as New Zealand's unofficial national anthem.

'Pokarekare Ana' has featured on many New Zealand music albums, but made most famous by Dame Kiri Te Kanawa.

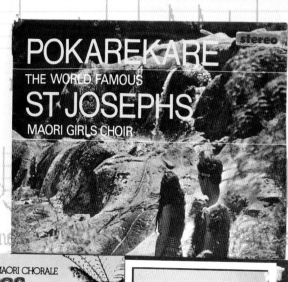

Holidays

The Bach

'Are we there yet?'

Although now endangered by up-market development and the high prices of beachfront property, the beach bach used to be (and often still remains) a uniquely Kiwi phenomenon. Because of New Zealand's island status, with relatively easy access to a coastline of some sort, the humble beach bach became regarded as a slice of paradise in Godzone. Never mind the fact that such 'second residences' were often thrown together (even old-world architects had unprepossessing dwellings) using wooden packing boxes, car cases, basic fibrolite and corrugated iron. Some even utilised the rugged shells of old trams and abandoned railway carriages.

Clarry's bach on the Coromandel Peninsula, for example, started life as an old car crate. A corrugated iron roof was attached sometime before World War II. After the war Clarry

Opposite: Baches at Jacks Bay, the Catlins, 1964.

returned pretty much shot up and on the lookout for a place of retreat and rehabilitation. Clarry retreated on the weekends, and, still the handyman, set about extending the bach beyond its basic beginnings.

It seems appropriate that the word itself, bach, is truncated and basic. It is believed to have started life as 'bachelor accommodation', reflecting the famous 'man alone' image of New Zealand males living in Spartan but unencumbered circumstances. Just like the pioneers. To confuse the history, though, South Islanders call their retreats 'cribs', originating from Charles Dickens' use of the word in *Oliver Twist*, in reference to a lodging or public house.

Clarry's bach was, come to think of it, a bit like a public house at times. Nearby blokes who came to help him assemble the extensions stayed on for a few beers and a yarn. So much so that Clarry almost forgot about the war. In the end the car case hovel was extended into a more livable, L-shaped retreat, without losing its knocked up, lived-in and approachable charm.

The bach was seen as an emblem of the egalitarian society, but even in the 1960s factors like inflation took the acquisition of such routine seaside shelters away from the 'average' New Zealander.

The true, 'humble' bach often contained cast-off furniture, sofas with suspect springs, rickety bunks, perhaps a small fridge and, more often than not, a smaller stove that was as slow as it was inadequate, particularly when the entire family bunked down.

But Kiwis loved their baches and the 'are we there yet?' exhortations of impatient offspring were all about the excitement of getting to the beach — and the bach.

Bach at Te Hatepe, near Taupo, 1984.

Caravan and Camp-o-matic

A home away from home on wheels

If the small North King Country town of Otorohanga is now famous for its Kiwi House and Kiwiana collection, it was for many years known as the base for some of New Zealand's most hardy and stylish caravan construction.

In the wake of the early 1960s' prosperity in New Zealand, caravan ownership became popular. Now that many of the roads had been tarsealed and widened, it was appropriate to hitch up the caravan and make a beeline for the coast. The caravan, of course, during the easy years of the 1960s could be a status symbol, but more often than not it was simply an adjunct to the annual holidays. It was better than bunking down in a tent.

If you didn't like the 'neighbours' at one camping ground, or the surf was down and the weather foul, you could move to another. That kept often bored kids on their toes, the business of shifting camp. The caravan provided security too — of sorts. You could lock the door, although on hot summer nights all windows would be thrown open, letting in cool sea breezes and sandflies, mosquitoes and other intruders.

With a caravan as opposed to a tent, you didn't trip over guy ropes, and although caravans had the propensity to occasionally float away in summer flash floods, they were better able to withstand lashing wind storms and rain bombs than tents were.

At a time when 'keeping up with the Joneses' rather cocked a snook at New Zealand's famous egalitarianism (or confirmed it) a caravan was less

Caravan on the Taranaki coast.

the one-time holiday settings were given over to more itinerant Kiwis as cheap accommodation options. Bad tenant reputations sometimes developed within the thin walls of an invention that had set out from home with good intentions.

Caravanning in New Zealand began in the 1920s and burgeoned in the post-World War II years until their production and usage peaked in the 1970s. The most influential of New Zealand's early caravan makers was Tanners Trailers, based in Eden Terrace, Auckland. After World War II, Munro of Otorohanga, Liteweight of Hamilton and Zephyr of Dunedin provided stiff competition and caravan clubs were established in the major cities. Anglo Trail-Lite and Oxford were among new companies that pumped out caravans in the following years, to help feed a demand that in 1963 reached 2000 new caravans sold annually. By the end of the 1960s, New Zealand's economy was beginning to buckle, yet the caravan craze continued, almost as if the caravan represented a denial of the end of the golden weather — those prosperous post-war years that would soon see the sun rise on recession.

In 1979 Robert Muldoon's National government suddenly unleashed a 20 percent sales tax on caravans and the industry took a nose dive. Most manufacturers went out of

pretentious than booking the whole family into one of the new motels springing up along the coast, as if this was New Jersey, USA. Most caravans were modest enough with sleeping provision for half a dozen people, once the communal table had been folded away and squabs realigned.

As caravans became more common, permanent sites were set up at camping grounds and wheels removed. Trailer parks and caravan enclosures developed along American lines. Soon business within weeks.

In a changing New Zealand where it was no longer possible for everyone to keep up with the Joneses, the caravan landscape soon featured extremes. The Lilliput, which in its original form was only 9 feet long and 6 feet wide, compared starkly with the likes of the large, four-wheeled Luxliners built by Modern Caravans. The original modus operandi of the caravan — that of getting away from it all, including all those mod cons of the 1960s — was often turned on its ear as 'holidaymakers' installed TV sets, microwave ovens and stereos in their large ostentatious homes away from home.

In response to the collapse of the caravan market in the 1980s, mutations like the Caravette, a folding caravan that could be towed by a motorbike, and 'pop-tops' like the Camp-o-matic and the Liteweight Expander emerged. The latter two were a compressed box on wheels that housed a fibreglass roof and aluminium sides and could be converted readily into what looked for all the world like a small conventional caravan. Campervans developed too in response to changing economic times.

In recent years, with bach ownership falling outside the ambit of many Kiwis, caravans have made a welcome return.

Train Travel

Get me to the beach on time

Before cars and highways became the standard way of getting away on holiday — invariably to the beach — train travel featured prominently. It was not uncommon for land-locked central North Island families to catch the Wellington to Auckland express, connect with the Opua Express

An 'excursion special' in 1908, one kilometre west of Waiouru.

at the end of the Main Trunk, and end up in the Bay of Islands. Or catch a mixed goods with carriage attached to Hamilton's Frankton Junction, before linking with the Taneatua Express which steamed out across the eastern Waikato Plains, through the Karangahake and Athenree Gorges, before alighting at Tauranga on the coast.

In the very early days, the Railways Department encouraged passengers with colourful posters relating to 'exotic' destinations like Lake Wakatipu, along the Invercargill to Kingston line, the steaming wonderland Rotorua from Auckland on the prestigious Rotorua Limited along the Rotorua branch, and the Waitomo Caves via the North Island Main Trunk.

Highway development made redundant much of the need for train travel. After all there were no railway lines leading to many of the Coromandel Peninsula beaches that could now be accessed by circuitous and dusty roads.

But for younger Kiwis, those who were often encouraged to travel on their own in a social climate that was as safe as houses (apart from the occasional main trunk drunk on the expresses who would simply ask you for money and breathe fumes), train trips in the holidays became a standard means of travelling before kids were old enough or their parents sufficiently wealthy to finance them into their first car.

These days holidays and train travel are inter-linked with the tourist trade and the specialist long-distance rail adventures provided by KiwiRail: the TranzAlpine from coast to coast in the South Island — Christchurch to Greymouth, the TranzCoastal, a superior maritime journey up the coast between Christchurch and Picton, and the Overlander, Auckland to Wellington. It has been said that a journey on any of these trains constitutes a holiday in itself. The trains of earlier decades were far less luxurious and lacked the on-board dining facilities of the current long-distance trains.

The refreshment stop was an integral aspect of train travel, and the stampede to the railway refreshment rooms was part of New Zealand folklore. In exchange for brimming cups of hot tea and coffee, pies, ham sandwiches and slabs of fruit cake, passengers often received barked shins, scalded hands and chipped teeth. It was regarded as a small price to pay back then and remained as an indelible memory of what holiday train travel was like before cars, buses and planes took over.

Railways advertising in the 1940s.

Air Travel

The non-flightless Kiwi

New Zealand's first regular air service was a weekly flight between Dunedin and Christchurch in 1930. In the same year Dominion Airlines Ltd began operating on a daily basis between Hastings and Gisborne. In other parts of the country small operators offered regular services, although the motto 'one plane, one pilot' was largely adhered to.

New Zealand's first major airline, Union Airways of New Zealand Ltd, was registered in 1935. It was an arm of the Union Steam Ship Company and as early as 1913 had expressed an interest in extending its operations to aviation. However, it wasn't until 1936 that Union Airways provided New Zealand's first trunk service, flying between Palmerston North and Dunedin, with intermediate stops at Blenheim and Christchurch. A link was provided for passengers wishing to transfer to Wellington as well. From Blenheim, Cook Strait Airways flew across the channel to the capital.

Union may have not been a 'one plane, one pilot' operation, but its fleet of three De Havilland 86 express airliners was modest enough. When two all-metal Lockheed Electras were added in 1937, Union Airways was able to really get off the ground. An Auckland to Wellington flight proved popular enough in its first six months of operation to attract 4,496 passengers. Kiwis were beginning to lose their flightless tag.

After World War II the stylish way to travel to Australia, the Pacific Islands and eventually America was aboard the flying boat. From Musick Point in Auckland, immaculately suited men and admirably coiffeured women would alight the flying boats of Pan American World Airways before being airlifted elsewhere.

In the years between the flying boats and the advent of the jet airliner, Kiwis heading overseas favoured cruise liners: purpose-built ships that provided an uplifting experience as they moved steadily towards their destination — usually Sydney, Melbourne, or perhaps one of the Pacific Islands.

While it had been possible previously to fly across the Tasman, until the advent of the Douglas DC-8 in 1965 (Air New Zealand's first jet airliner) the prospect of instant holidays in Australia had never been contemplated. In the years after the Beatle invasion and the subsequent youth revolution, jet travel transformed New Zealanders' aspirations regarding holidays. Suddenly, it was possible to get from Auckland to Sydney in three hours.

The DC-8, the pioneering craft, was succeeded by the three-engined DC-10 and before too long the actual jumbo jet, the Boeing 747, increased travel options and range of destinations.

By the 1970s thousands of young New Zealanders were travelling to Britain, Europe and the USA. The Overseas Experience ('OE') had been sanctified. New Zealand's remote location at the bottom of the world meant that more Kiwis took to the skies than many other nationalities. The fact that Britain, in particular, was still regarded as the land of our forefathers and mothers enticed younger generations — and eventually pre-baby-boomers — to take advantage of the new long-range jet airliners.

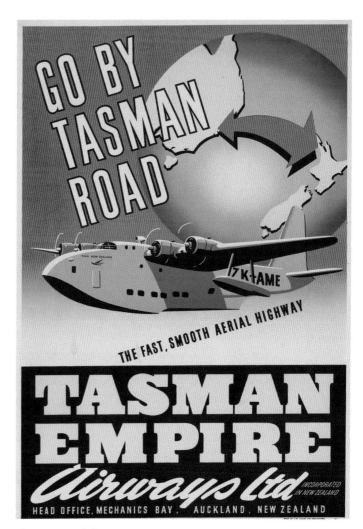

The cover of the Tasman Empire Airways Limited menu, 1946.

Opo

Cavorting in the 1950s shallows

In this day and age the phenomenon of a friendly dolphin cavorting in the shallows with kids (as happened in recent years at Mahia with 'Moko' the dolphin), inevitably set off politically correct reactions regarding the inalienable rights and safety of the dolphin. Back in the summer of 1955–56, 'Opo', a friendly bottlenose dolphin that cavorted in much the same way with humans at Opononi on the Hokianga Harbour, produced a groundswell of bonhomie and feel-good factors. Thousands of holidaymakers scheduled Opononi into their summer holiday itinerary as the spectacle and reputation of Opo increased. In an island nation surrounded by sea the connection between the friendly dolphin and Kiwis took on a symbolic, even spiritual, significance. During the 'Golden Weather Years' of the 1950s when New Zealand was often regarded as one of the best places to live, we felt privileged to have 'Opo' come ashore and confirm our paradise status.

Pat McMinn, a Rosemary Clooney clone and New Zealand's Queen of Popular Music in the mid-50s, recorded a local composition, 'Opo the Crazy Dolphin'. The song became the hit of the year in 1955. Pat McMinn, Bill Langford and the Crombie Murdoch Trio, the musical team responsible for the song, wrote and recorded it in a single day. Just as the tape arrived at the radio station for its debut airing, the news of Opo's passing came through.

Opo was found dead, stranded in a rock pool, and the nation mourned. Perhaps we should have taken greater care of her. Now in the car park outside the Opononi Resort Hotel, you will find a statue of Opo. Her grave is located next door near the local War Memorial Hall.

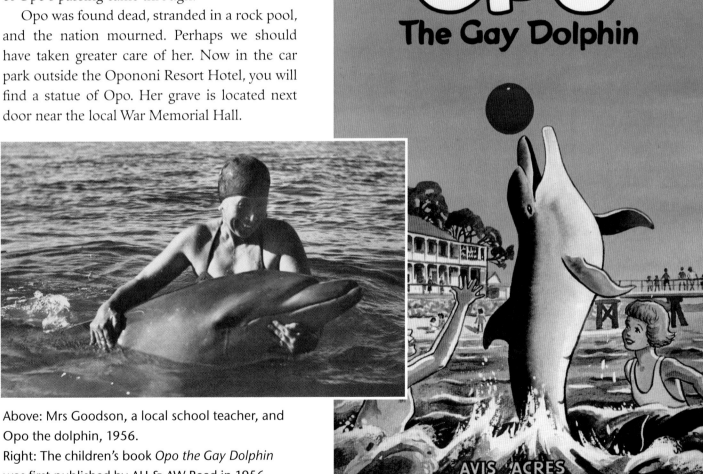

Above: Mrs Goodson, a local school teacher, and Opo the dolphin, 1956.
Right: The children's book *Opo the Gay Dolphin* was first published by AH & AW Reed in 1956.

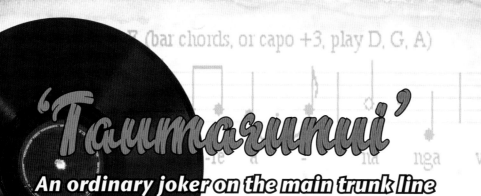

'Taumarunui'

An ordinary joker on the main trunk line

When New Zealand Railways were in their heyday and the Auckland to Wellington Express was just about the most famous of the long-distance passenger services, central North Island towns like Taihape, Te Kuiti and Taumarunui had a distinct character. These were the towns, located at strategic distances along the Main Trunk Line, that were as well known for their nurturance of the many trains that passed through, day and night, as they were for their servicing function in support of agriculture, timber industries and anything else that needed servicing.

More than anything, though, particularly in the decades between the opening of the Main Trunk in 1908 and the decline of rail travel, they were regarded as railway towns. Steam engines needed a lot of sustenance in their battles with the rugged terrain. The railway towns provided watering and refuelling facilities, maintenance and crew changes. Often fresh engines were required — or extra units to assist the leading engine. Hundreds of passengers needed sustenance too. Towns like Taihape, Te Kuiti and Taumarunui provided 'time for refreshments' in bustling refreshment rooms that required the hungry, thirsty or just plain sleepless hordes to leave the comparative comfort of their carriage seats and walk, run or stumble along the platform to the brightly lit serveries. They would be rewarded with pies, sandwiches and buns, and steaming cups of tea or coffee before having to negotiate their way back through swirling crowds and often freezing temperatures, in the knowledge that time was not on their side. There was no time to dally as the express prepared to depart.

Peter Cape captured the essence of a ritual that became part and parcel of train travel in New Zealand when he wrote 'Taumarunui' in 1958. It was the first song for which Cape wrote both the words and music, although Pat Rogers, a Wellington tram driver, was later to record it with its more recognisable tune — written by Rogers himself. The original tune by Cape was considered to be too wide-ranging for Pat Rogers' vocal range.

Tony Vercoe of Kiwi Records, while taking a shine to Peter Cape's first song, didn't think he was up to singing it on record. Subsequently, the 'professional' musician Pat Rogers was whistled up. The Pat Rogers version was released in 1959 on an extended-play 45 called 'New Zealand Vernacular Ballads'. The record also included 'Bullocky', another Peter Cape song, and two Pat Rogers compositions, 'Young Kiwi' and 'Sheep Cocky'. It was appropriate it should be released on Kiwi Records.

'Taumarunui' not only rejoiced in the Kiwi vernacular of the time, it told a story. With expressions like 'I'm an ordinary joker', 'there's a sheila in refreshments', 'my heart jumps like a rabbit', 'she's got hair a flaming yellow, a mouth a flaming red' and 'I thought that she'd be jake', Cape unravelled his tale of woe. Or rather that of a woebegone Kiwi joker who,

while travelling on the overnight train and visiting the refreshment rooms of Taumarunui, fell hopelessly in love with one of the station's tea-pourers. He became so enamoured that he tried to find work in the town in the hope that he'd be able to make advances. When he found jobs hard to come by he trained up as a fireman on the nocturnal Limited Express, knowing the train stopped nightly for ten minutes. Ten minutes was better than nothing when

you're desperate and smitten. Then in a cruel twist the tea-pouring sheila, unimpressed by the amorous fireman, changed to the daylight shift. The fireman no longer had even ten minutes' access to her.

The song struck a chord in a New Zealand that was still coming to terms with the serious business of laughing at itself. It's surprising now to learn that when the song was released and become popular many citizens of Taumarunui felt offended by some of the song's insinuations. The bit about not being able to get a job in Taumarunui came in for criticism. Not surprisingly, the girls who worked at the station's refreshment rooms didn't like it much either.

Times change. In 1993 when Taumarunui hosted a 'Steam Festival' event, celebrating the history of the railway, the song was treated as a

The railway station refreshment room, this time in Christchurch, 1952.

virtual anthem. Not only were locals and visitors laughing at the song's inherent humour, as it was sung again and again, but its rendition was attended by a certain reverence.

'Taumarunui' and other Peter Cape compositions like 'She'll be Right' and 'Down the Hall on Saturday Night', helped define Pakeha culture at a time when Kiwis were groping for a distinctive New Zealand identity. Despite local grumbles from Taumarunui folk, it was surprising how readily the song was accepted for what it was: a laconic, tuneful and accurate depiction of something uniquely Kiwi. It hit the spot. Cape himself commented in 1962 that finally New Zealanders were beginning to laugh at themselves. The contribution of 'Taumarunui' played a part in that process.

'Taumarunui' is rightly regarded as a classic New Zealand folk song. It was so ear-catching that it travelled across the Tasman where a local adaptation, called 'Cootamundra', was virtually identical, apart from the obvious need to change place names to render it a 'genuine' Australian song. And Peter Cape received further recognition as an outstanding song writer when an American folk singer named Gordon Bok recorded 'The Stable Lad', another Peter Cape original.

Rural Life

Fred Dagg

'Get in behind'

Even as New Zealand became more urbanised in the 1960s and 1970s, factors like Barry Crump's books — invariably yarnish and set in the great outdoors — and a bolt from the green with multi-media TV personality Fred Dagg (aka John Clarke) aroused something in the Kiwi psyche and funny bone. Perhaps we were uncomfortable with becoming city slickers. Certainly, the sense of nostalgia attached to an uncomplicated life down on the farm appealed as city life became intense and often complicated.

A romanticised notion of life on the land emerged in New Zealand during the years comedian Fred Dagg (with a surname like that he had to be a man of the sheep rearing land) captured our imaginations. A command to 'rattle your dags' became pure Kiwi as a plea to get a move on. 'Get in behind' and 'Get away back' were rural commands similarly popularised by Dagg.

Fred Dagg, with shaggy hair beneath a broad-rimmed hat, mandatory black singlet, unflattering shorts and perennial gumboots, came into Kiwi homes via TV, radio, records and books. With his parodies of the 'Kiwi bloke' and laconic one-liners, tempered by 70s world views, Dagg struck a ringing chord. Early on he appeared in one of New Zealand's most enduring and endearing TV programmes, *Country Calendar*, sitting around the farmhouse breakfast table with his seven sons, all called Trevor. Traditional quart bottles of beer were not so much drizzled as gurgled on to the morning cereal as the rural day awoke.

Later Fred Dagg featured in his own programme and became as well known as the Prime Minister, before sneaking off to Australia, one assumes, in gumboots and black singlet.

John Morrison Clarke, Dagg's creator, was born in Palmerston North in 1948. He cut his dramatic teeth in the Victoria University

revue of 1969 before appearing in a revue at Downstage Theatre in Wellington. In the early 1970s he worked for a time in London and, back home, made his first TV appearance in *Gallery*, a current affairs programme, in 1973.

He rapidly became a favourite — a phenomenon really — of New Zealand comedy. As well as his regular TV appearances, he toured the country in a stage show, made a movie called *Dagg Day Afternoon* and his records included the best-selling *Fred Dagg's Greatest Hits* (1975). Thirty years after its release, this album remains one of New Zealand's all time best-selling records.

Fred Dagg in a singlet especially embroidered for him by a fan.

Sheep

Providing warmth and sustenance

New Zealand is famous for sheep. Mention New Zealand in Europe and the USA and the response you get will invariably be 'That's near Australia, isn't it?' and 'It has lots of sheep.'

Captain Cook is credited with releasing a ram and a ewe in the Marlborough Sounds, but they appeared to have disappeared without trace. The idea was that sheep would provide wool for clothing and meat for sustenance in the new colony. The Reverend Samuel Marsden was similarly unsuccessful when he released a small flock of Merinos, some 20 years later, although the first successful colony of sheep was a flock of Merinos on Mana Island in 1834.

From such humble beginnings, sheep proliferated. The New Zealand environment, at last, suited them and before too long sheep farming was established and wool became one of the country's first export earners. With the establishment of refrigerated shipping in 1886,

FIRST PRIZE

the export of sheep carcasses, principally to Great Britain, saw sheep meat exports burgeon. Merinos were joined by Romney and other breeds, including Coopworth, New Zealand Halfbred, Perendale and Corriedale.

Meanwhile, wool exports represented 75 percent of the new colony's exports in the 1860s and went on to become New Zealand's longest running export item.

In the 1980s sheep numbers topped 70 million. Now reduced to almost half that number, sheep are still a dominant presence on typically rugged and rolling landscapes. On the back of sheep and its wool/meat dominance in the Kiwi lifestyle, iconic activities like knitting emerged with women producing home-made garments, while travelling on trains, boats and buses, or sitting around the open fire. Multi-tasking in New Zealand began with knitting, for women were able to co-ordinate their knitting while carrying on conversations and/or listening to the radio and issuing domestic commands.

There are more sheep than people in New Zealand and their preponderance has led to further spin-offs. Sheep shearing has become a bona fide competition sport and since a man named Godfrey Bowen sheared 463 sheep in a nine-hour record-setting effort in 1961, competitions like the 'Golden Shears' and shearing champions like the Fagan brothers of Te Kuiti have continued to boost shearing as a sport, and individuals have set new records.

Te Kuiti presents itself as the shearing capital of the world, a point emphasised by a large statue of a shearer at the southern approaches to the town. The same centre now parades an annual 'running of the sheep' event, when a large number of the woolly beasts are released to scamper through the town to the considerable delight of locals and tourists.

Tourists from countries like Japan, where sheep are few on the ground, delight in watching and taking snaps of sheep flocks in rural recesses. More formalised tourist operators feature sheep being put through their paces in enclosed settings like Rotorua's Agrodome and Northland's SheepWorld.

For Kiwis, sheep continue to provide wool for warm clothing and blankets, and in terms of sustenance, many families still enjoy the once-common Sunday meal staple — roast mutton or lamb with all the trimmings.

New Zealand's most famous All Black, Colin Meads, was raised on a sheep farm and is reported to have eaten mutton three times a day: mutton chops for breakfast, cold cuts for lunch and an evening meal of roast lamb or mutton.

Corrugated Iron

'As Kiwi as . . .'

Corrugated iron was initially imported into New Zealand but in 1869 local manufacture of the 'ripple effect' iron began. Soon the galvanising process was done locally too and thus New Zealand had a ready supply of a critical rust-resistant roofing material. Typically, Kiwis used corrugated iron for other purposes as well including fences, outhouses, beach baches, chicken coops, dog kennels, chimneys, water tanks and the iconic red woolshed and kids' tree huts.

'As Kiwi as corrugated iron' became a popular saying and certainly the distinctive rippled iron became a common building material. Amazingly, it had been rejected as a preferred building iron in England, where it was considered suitable only for fences and temporary buildings.

Perhaps there was something in the emergence of a distinct Kiwi identity that led to the glorification of corrugated iron in the new country — away from Mother England who had turned her nose up at the 'inferior' material.

As a roofing iron it was suitable for our ample rainfall, making it run in more regulated fashion towards spouting. The corrugations provided strength, so there was less tendency to buckle and pond than with flat iron.

Corrugated iron was in short supply during World War II and tile and bitumen roofs gained ground. Corrugated iron also lost out during the splurge of house building in the 1950s and 1960s, when it was regarded as rather common. Was it our English ancestry and latent snobbery emerging when 'Decramastic' roofs became popular?

In recent years wearable art festivals have featured corrugated iron skirts, bras and full body armour and an artist named Jeff Thomson, suitably inspired by the utilisation of the rumpled iron in the rural landscape, has created numerous corrugated iron sculptures. It has been his riveted depictions of cows that have proved most popular. Corrugated iron cows are about as 'Kiwi' as an object can get — unless it was the shield, shaped like the famous Ranfurly Shield, which was forged out of corrugated iron to reward the winner of minor but strenuous rugby matches among bush-country shearers.

Footrot Flats

A slice of heaven

In 1975, not long after the Fred Dagg phenomenon, a cartoon series called *Footrot Flats* was first published in New Zealand newspapers and magazines. Cartoonist Murray Ball, its creator, was the son of an All Black and a fair player himself, having represented Manawatu and the Junior All Blacks. Obviously, the pivotal rugby component of rural life was represented as Ball won the hearts of all Kiwis, rural, urban or expatriate. A dog named Dog was the central character and many amusing and heart-warming sketches adorned syndicated papers throughout New Zealand and Australia, as well as in Scandinavia and other unlikely reaches as well.

The cartoon was set on the farm of Wal Footrot, a sheep farmer, and while Dog was the central focus, there were other memorable main actors. Socrates 'Cooch' Windgrass was Wal's neighbour, Darlene 'Cheeky' Hobson, his girlfriend, Rangi Wiremu Waka Jones was a local who helped out on the farm and Janice 'Pongo' Footrot was Wal's niece. Then there was Dolores Monrovia Godwit 'Aunt Dolly' Footrot and Horse, a large, fierce cat.

Astoundingly, for a popular print media cartoon that seemed one-dimensional in terms of its apparent appeal, *Footrot Flats* was adapted and propelled to stage show and animated movie status. The latter featured a song 'A Slice of Heaven', written and sung by Dave Dobbyn, which has legitimate claim to being New Zealand's grassroots national anthem should the position ever be up for grabs.

The cartoon strip peaked, in terms of popularity, in the 1980s, a time when the *Footrot Flats* books sold in their millions in Australasia. In 1994 the newspaper cartoons ceased, although previously unpublished strips continued to be released in book form until 2000. Murray Ball cited various reasons for winding up the cartoon. The death of his own dog was one, although more generalised disaffections, like the direction of New Zealand politics, cropped up.

Two collectors editions have been published: *Footrot Flats: The Dog Strips* and *Footrot Flats: The Long Weekender*. Inevitably, they were both bestsellers.

'Ten Guitars'

A B-side besides

'Ten Guitars' was written by Gordon Mills, the man responsible for managing Tom Jones and Engelbert Humperdinck, Britain's two 'big balladeers' in the 1960s. Mills was formerly the harmonica player for Jones and had already displayed his song-writing skills with unusual ballads like 'It's Not Unusual', by Tom Jones.

'Ten Guitars' became a Kiwi party sing-along favourite in the mid-60s, after it was discovered lurking on the B-side of Engelbert Humperdinck's chart-topping 'Release Me' single, a song successful enough to keep the Beatles off the top of the charts. 'Release Me' was popular enough but 'Ten Guitars' struck a chord with New Zealanders. Perhaps it was the 'Maori strum', a distinctive guitar style, that tweaked local ears, but more likely it was the communal nature of the lyrics and an uncomplicated yet compelling sing-along chorus that led to its popularity downunder.

The notion of ten guitarists at one party was considered a figure worthy of the challenge, although usually a lone guitarist held pride of place beside the barbecue, hangi or beer keg.

'I have a band of men and all they do is play for me. They come from miles around to hear me play a melody.' Such lines were a summons to a celebration and at a time when the Beatles' 'Strawberry Fields Forever' presented sometimes impenetrable 'progressive rock', 'Ten Guitars' was readily accessible.

In a remarkably short time, wherever there was a guitar (or several), a guitarist (or two), a ready supply of beer and Kiwi celebrants, 'Ten Guitars' was often the first song off the rank, and the last, and usually many times in between. In trains, at bus stations, in pubs, at the rugby after-match, or at the rugby itself, the distinctive Maori strum of the song's introduction became a constant.

'Dance, dance, dance to my ten guitars, and very soon you'll know just where you are . . .' went the chorus. It was vaguely cosmic, in keeping with the spiritual and spatial searching of the 1960s and 1970s, but there was little embarrassment. After all, the song suggested that if you danced and sang to the ten guitars, you could consider yourself grounded. You knew where 'you are' — New Zealand. Often it was rural-based, but it soon became small town, big city, at the beach, at birthday parties, New Year's Eve . . . Everyone knew where they were and most of them knew the words.

Soon local lyrical adaptations had the chorus ending with 'When you hula, hula, hula to my ten guitars', which rendered the song even more Polynesian and seemingly local. By this time 'Ten Guitars' had become overexposed. Bob Dylan, the Beatles and others were offering more wordy and philosophical ponderings, but 'Ten Guitars' still had its place. At parties where gathering interpersonal storms and misunderstandings increased, as the summer of love degenerated into winters of hard rain, the familiar chunking chords and bonding chorus of 'Ten Guitars' generated a united front.

Shopping

Farmers Trading Company

Of free trolley buses and Santa's claws

When the giant Santa Claus figure, which used to be anchored to the side of the Farmers, Hobson Street store in Auckland, became a media item in 2007 (the beckoning Santa finger was reputedly causing noise pollution), it drew attention to New Zealand's largest department store. A little grease fixed the problem and the winking-eyed Santa recommenced attracting Christmas shoppers to the country's most distinctive shopping precinct.

The Farmers Trading Company began life upstream as Laidlaw Leeds. Robert Laidlaw, its founder, produced mail order catalogues in 1910, two years after the opening of the North Island Main Trunk railway line became an important development in the transport of ordered goods. Goods like groceries, crockery and hardware could be moved more quickly from warehouse to buyer.

Catalogues continued to be produced until 1938, but long before that, in 1918, Laidlaw Leeds had merged with the Farmers Union Trading Company to form the Farmers Trading Company. In the early 1920s the first of their new department stores opened. Auckland's Hobson Street store was the flag-bearer after starting life as a warehouse in 1914, and remained New Zealand's largest department store until closing in 1991.

In 1922 a free trolley bus service and children's playground on the roof were opened. Because Hobson Street was an awkward walking

Opposite: The Farmers Christmas Parade passes in front of the giant Santa in 1983.

distance from the commercial retail hub of Queen Street, the trolley bus became an iconic convenience that attracted thousands. This and the kids' playground marked the 'Farmers' as New Zealand's most innovative retail outlet.

In 1930 the Auckland store opened the 'Help-Yourself Grocerteria' which, in 1952, became the 'Self-Service Food Hall'. Further innovations had seen the arrival in New Zealand of self-service.

In 1955 escalators attracted more shoppers and, in a concession to New Zealand's increasing car ownership, Auckland's first multi-storey carpark was opened in 1957 adjacent to the Hobson Street store.

For families of the 1950s and 1960s, a visit to Farmers, Hobson Street, was a highlight of a trip to the 'big smoke', Auckland. For kids, a free trip on the quiet, ghosting trolley bus was a good start, but then there were the escalator rides, before being left to your own devices on the rooftop playground, while Mum and Dad shopped unencumbered.

Farmers, Hobson Street, was a revelation in a time of somewhat sober retail practices. And to think that Laidlaw Leeds, the precursor company, had in 1918 advertised products like Comstocks Worm Pellets, Dr. Sheldon's Magnetic Liniment and Dingo Toothache Remedy. To teenagers of the 1960s, such items would have seemed like names of psychedelic rock bands from San Francisco as they mooched around the pedal car enclosure on the roof, trawled the record bars and lingerie emporiums and rode the escalators on their own, in a state of mild euphoria.

Four Square

Not for squares

General stores, now a novelty on the landscape and usually associated with tiny backwaters and hamlets, were once a common sight in New Zealand.

The chain store became a threat in the 1920s, as the homely goodwill of general store owners was put to the sword. Local loyalties held the line, however, and what was later known as the Four Square Group emerged, an association whereby combined buying power helped keep prices down.

While Four Square was evolving, New Zealand had several grocery chain stores. In Auckland there were the Blue and White stores, Self Help Co-Op Ltd, Farmers' Trading Company, Hutchinson Brothers, and Marriotts Stores. The South Island had the Star Stores chain.

The origins of the name Four Square were straightforward and innocent enough, although in the 60s when to be judged 'square' was 'uncool' the name received derisory remarks from teenagers. In 1924 the company secretary, while checking and highlighting his calendar, placed a square around the 4th of July and in a white hot moment declared '4 Square' to be the name of the combined association of groceries.

By the early 1930s Four Square had increased its membership to over 100 stores. 'Self service', an American development, was introduced to Four Square stores in 1948, presaging the modus operandi of the supermarket. Two years later Four Square, with 700 stores, was able to make the claim of being 'The Dominion's largest grocery chain'.

Another iconic figure, 'Mr 4', the cartoon picture of the smiling grocer with hair parted towards the middle, a thumbs-up gesture and a pencil wedged rakishly behind a clean ear (a Kiwi habit rather like the sunglasses resting on top of the head of recent years) emerged as Four Square continued to thrive.

By the time the chain hit the 1000 mark in 1956, it was already a Kiwi icon. A quartet of Christchurch

folk musicians changed their name from the Southern Yeoman to the Four Squares, as much to cash in on the familiar name of the grocery near you, as to introduce a sense of ironic humour at a time when James Dean and Elvis Presley were promoting anti-'square' gestures. 'Square'-bashing it was called, before Dean died in a car crash and Presley was drafted into the army.

The bedding in of the supermarket threatened Four Square during the 1960s, who kept their heads above water by touting speed and efficiency. Four Square became innovative, certainly not 'square'. As well as speed and efficiency for the customer's benefit, elaborate competitions were staged. In 1962, 'Check-It' was regarded as New Zealand's biggest commercial competition. Prizes like TV sets and cars ('Minis for Mum') were up for grabs. Every 4th of July, Four Square's birthday, all babies born on the same date received prizes. Multiple births did even better — a Vauxhall Velox for triplets, a new fridge for twins. Four Square survives in the twenty-first century, under the banner of the Foodstuffs conglomerate.

The ever-popular Four Square: a cookbook from the late 1960s and tea towel from today.

Corner Dairy

Oasis in the suburban desert

Corner dairies were invariably on corners, although many weren't. They tended to pop up in the most unlikely locations in suburban, city or small town settings. Usually located where shopping centres weren't, the corner dairy was often like an oasis in a relentless suburban desert.

Traditional corner dairies often occupied two storey buildings with provision for the husband and wife operators to live on the premises. Often Indian couples and their broods of offspring ran in and out of gaps between advertising displays and freezer units.

The corner dairy sold everything, although prices were less competitive than the fully fledged grocery or supermarket in town. It became a very Kiwi activity to wander down to the corner dairy, after you'd arrived home from the teeming city, or in the weekend, to pick up a pack of fags or a bottle of milk, a loaf of bread and other staples that had run out. Sunday papers were another popular item available from the corner dairy that required little more than a casual saunter in the Sunday sun or a short, sharp sprint between New Zealand's famous isolated showers.

Power shopping it wasn't. Bare-topped blokes in jandals, women in hair curlers, even in dressing gowns were known to wander into the corner dairy.

In the 1950s and 1960s as the new suburbs extended into rural areas beyond the old city boundaries, the often new, sterile suburbs, nesting

THE LONGEST

DRINK IN TOWN

grounds for the famous post-war baby-boom, presented a socially barren landscape for young mothers often labouring in 'Nappy Valley' on their own. The daily amble down to the corner dairy was as much for a 'humanity fix' and a chat with the dairy owner and fellow customers as to make a handful of often random, sometimes unnecessary purchases — a tin of beetroot and perhaps an ice-cream for the kids.

The corner dairy even now serves such a social service. Some are now licensed to sell alcohol, which has added to their popularity. Of course, over the years new migrant dairy owners, with well-intentioned if faltering English, can no longer always provide the conversational support once provided as a by-product of shopping at the corner dairy.

Another recent development too has been the spate of often violent robberies perpetrated against the corner dairy, which in these matters have revealed their vulnerability to criminal opportunist elements of New Zealand's new underclass.

Corner dairies are often located near schools, where pupils used to drop in for a pie or packet of jaffas, before or after school. Before the days of chronic truancy (school kids drop in whenever they like now), the corner dairy was often a gathering place for school kids after school, where they'd top up with ice-cream, compare notes, and hang out with friends and suitors.

Some of our favourite dairy goodies: K-Bars, jet planes, jaffas, bananas and jelly beans.

138

Pie Cart

Give peas a chance

The humble meat pie, although it did not originate in New Zealand, became our most famous fast food item. It was around long before fast-food became common terminology. Mince was the standard filling, although the pie eventually came to encase many different fillings in its pastry sarcophagus.

It was eminently practical and convenient — a meal in itself that had the advantage of coming self-wrapped. You could eat a pie on the hoof, on the train, on the way to work, or at the rugby. Quality control wasn't always a concern in earlier times, although these days greater emphasis is placed on making a better product, in terms of nutritional value. The proliferation of fast-food options has forced the common pie to lift its game.

Earlier, some pies were stingy on the meat, generous on the lard-ladened pastry. Sometimes 'meat' pies seemed to contain little more than a

The great White Lady on the Auckland waterfront.

congealed deposit of gravy. Schoolboys delighted in telling fellow pie-munchers that the pies they had bought from a particular outlet were known to contain cat, dog, rat-tails and worse.

Because of the iconic status of the humble meat pie, it was inevitable that a place of purveyance would evolve. Pie carts, invariably converted caravans, some mobile, some permanent fixtures, developed to purvey pies and other food items. Based loosely on the American diner concept the pie cart presented a standard pie, pea and (s)pud sit-down meal in a humble alcove, but essentially they were takeaway providers. More than that they became the night-time flame that drew late-night moths — tipsy revellers, night-workers and drunken sports teams.

The modern pie cart: The Ponga Bar in Hahei.

Pie carts like Auckland's famous White Lady were critical late night rendezvous points for rugby fans taking the long way home. The White Lady's steak and eggs were as good as any top-of-the-range restaurant fare. As were the pies. Most cities and small towns boasted a pie cart, usually located in the centre of town, where a sense of bonhomie (and the occasional bout of fisticuffs) complemented sustaining and reviving late-night meals.

Back in the 1960s when pie carts were at their zenith, a certain innocence stalked New Zealand's streets. As a consequence, the names of some pie carts were somewhat risqué by today's PC standards. The White Lady was one thing but the owners of the 'Jigaboo' pie cart, utilising a put-down reference to US racial stereotyping, and the 'Gaytime Diner', located in another land-locked hamlet, were not to know of social developments in later decades.

Back in its heyday, the pie cart was risqué enough anyway. Parents warned their teenage offspring to avoid them. Not only was the food lacking in vegetables, but the clientele was often drunk and mind-warping. Because of such parental strictures pie carts became forbidden and enticing bases in the night, the place where a certain amount of 'action' unfolded and teenage

rebellion could be expressed. And the pies tasted better, particularly if they were purchased as 'dressed pies', a pie cart speciality. A mound of mashed potatoes and a squeeze of green peas would be mounted on a standard mince pie, rendering the pie 'dressed'. Parental criticism regarding the lack of vegetables at pie carts could be appeased, although many of the peas usually rolled away into the gutter before ingestion.

The White Lady attracts customers from all walks of life.

'We Don't Know How Lucky We Are'

'Yeah. Right, Fred'

'We Don't Know How Lucky We Are' was a song that summed up, somewhat laconically, New Zealand's apparent place in the sun. Its creator and singer, John Clarke, a.k.a. Fred Dagg, was nothing if not ironic. At a time when New Zealand was becoming increasingly urbanised and even the sacred quarter-acre section was being threatened by cross-leasing and land-less inner city redevelopment, Fred Dagg adopted a rural persona.

Some conservative farming elements were not too enamoured of Fred Dagg's mickey-taking, but urban New Zealand in particular warmed to the

John Clarke as Fred Dagg released three albums, *Fred Dagg's Greatest Hits* was a bestseller.

back-blocks philosophising of the floppy-hatted Dagg. The short-back-and-sides look was compromised by flowing 'hippie' locks beneath the hat, concealing male pattern baldness as much as it revealed a unique comedic talent.

After establishing his identity through TV cameos, Fred Dagg became a recording star as well. 'We Don't Know How Lucky We Are' was released in 1975 and reached number 17 in the charts. It featured in the New Zealand hit parade for four weeks. A song called 'Gumboots', released in the following year, did even better, cresting at number six and hanging around for an impressive 15 weeks. However, it was 'We Don't Know How Lucky We Are' that became embedded in Kiwi consciousness, with its simple tune, home-grown philosophy and mildly chastising tone.

New Zealand, by 1975, was in a certain amount of strife. The fallout from being cast adrift by Mother England, in trade terms, was impacting. Economically, we were in disrepair. Socially, several chickens were coming home to roost. As if to deny the looming clouds, 'We Don't Know How Lucky We Are' appeared to be confirmation of New Zealand's place in the sun. More serious, thoughtful types saw it as a harbinger of doom and gloom.

If we were that lucky how come Fred Dagg departed our shores for Australia in the late 1970s? Meanwhile, 'We Don't Know How Lucky We Are' continued to be sung lustily at pub sing-alongs and parties, with more emphasis on the positive, uplifting, confirming chorus than the tongue-in-cheek verses.

About the Author

Graham Hutchins has written many books on non-fiction subjects ranging from rugby, cricket, crime and rock music to railways, travel, trivia and New Zealand social history. He has also written works of fiction, including two novels with musical themes that were subsequently adapted for National Radio. All Graham's books have a strong Kiwi flavour, so a Kiwiana collection was a natural progression.